The Tax Smart Landlord

"Tax Smart" Strategies For Landlords To Save Thousands In Taxes Every Year

By Ted Lanzaro, CPA, Real Estate Broker

For information and other requests, please write:

Tax Smart Publishing, LLC
575 Highland Avenue
Cheshire, CT 06410
Or Call: 203-922-1742

You may also email orders and requests to:

ted@lanzarocpa.com

Printed in the United States of America

Disclaimer

Material presented in this publication is intended for informational purposes only. It is not intended as professional advice and should not be construed as such. Tax laws are subject to change. Tax reduction strategies need to be tailored to the specific tax situation of the individual or company using them.

The material in this publication is presented with the understanding and agreement that Tax Smart Publishing, LLC, and the author, Theodore D. Lanzaro, CPA, are not engaged in rendering legal, tax or other professional advice or services by publishing this material. The services of a competent professional should be sought if legal, tax, accounting, or other specific expert assistance is required.

Any unauthorized use of the material contained herein is at the user's own risk. Tax Smart Publishing, LLC, and Theodore D. Lanzaro, CPA, do not advocate the use of illegal tax devices or schemes. Many tax laws are not clear cut and there is no guarantee that any tax strategies discussed in this publication will be accepted by an IRS agent in an audit. Before using any of these strategies, you must consult a competent legal and tax professional and obtain specific expert assistance in implementing these strategies.

Also, these strategies are based on Federal tax laws as of the date of publication. These tax laws can change. State and local tax laws can vary. Please consult a tax professional in your locale about the legality of specific strategies as they relate to state or local tax laws.

Transmission of the information and material herein is not intended to create, and receipt does not constitute, an agreement to create an accountant-client relationship with Theodore D. Lanzaro, CPA, or Tax Smart Publishing, LLC.

This publication is not intended to constitute legal, tax or accounting advice or the provision of accounting and tax services. By publishing this book and its contents, neither Tax Smart Publishing, LLC, nor Theodore D. Lanzaro, CPA, intends to solicit tax and accounting business from clients located in states or jurisdictions where Theodore D. Lanzaro, CPA, is not licensed or authorized to provide accounting and tax services.

This publication may include links to resources of companies that assist real estate investors with tax and business related services. Neither Tax Smart Publishing, LLC, nor Theodore D. Lanzaro, CPA, necessarily sponsors, endorses or otherwise approves of these resources. Use them at your own risk.

Table of Contents

Copyright© 2018 by Theodore D. Lanzaro

WHY BE A "TAX SMART" LANDLORD?

This publication is designed for real estate investors – landlords involved in buying, leasing or selling residential and commercial real estate. If this is you, then you have in your hands a comprehensive, "plain English" guide to tax reduction strategies written specifically for real estate investors. This updated edition incorporates the Tax Cuts and Jobs Act of 2017 which took effect January 1, 2018. This major legislation brought in a wide range of changes to the tax codes and how they impact both corporations and individuals, including real estate investors. This revised edition will help the reader understand how to maximize tax savings on real estate investments using the new laws. As a real estate landlord, you may spend more money on taxes than on any other expense. You probably spend more on taxes than you do on housing, insurance, food, transportation, and utilities. The money you spend on taxes allows your local, state and Federal government to provide services to you. But, **you do not get any better service by paying more than you need to**. In fact, all you end up doing is paying more than your fair share of the burden of providing these services.

Most tax books and articles are written by college professors. I am not an academic. I am one of you, a real estate investor, as well as an experienced Certified Public Accountant and real estate broker. I will give you the information you need to save thousands of dollars annually on your taxes and do it in an easy, straightforward manner.

As a real estate landlord, you may spend more money on taxes than any other expense. You probably spend more on taxes than you do on housing, insurance, food, transportation or utilities. Your tax dollars allow your local, state and Federal government to provide services to you. But you do not get better services by paying more than you need to. All you end up doing is paying more than your fair share of the burden of providing these same services.

In fact, it is almost impossible to build wealth quickly without minimizing the amount of taxes you pay. Bill Gates, founder of Microsoft, and one of the richest men in the world, attributes much of his wealth to his working knowledge of tax law. This guide will give you the tools you need to implement and safeguard the strategies that will minimize your annual tax liability and help you build wealth from your real estate investments. Simply stated, the less in taxes you pay, the more money you have left over to re-invest and create wealth.

You might think that your accountant is already doing this for you. You would be incorrect! Most accountants do not have the necessary real estate industry experience to help you proactively to reduce your income taxes. Most likely, all your accountant is doing for you is filling out tax forms with the information you provide him. In my experience, this "reactive model" is how 90% of real estate landlords have their taxes prepared by their accountant.

Expecting your accountant to get you the most tax effective treatment on all aspects of your real estate landlord business is like expecting your doctor to maintain your body in excellent working condition. To do that, it would be necessary for him to be with you 24 hours a day, seven days a week, reminding you what to eat, how much to exercise, how long to sleep, etc. It is up to you as a real estate investor to be proactive and use the knowledge you will get from this guide to implement tax strategies that will allow you to minimize your taxes and build wealth.

Additionally, this guide will give you the tools and knowledge you need to keep the necessary records to safeguard your tax returns. Better record keeping helps your accountant prepare your taxes more accurately and document your income and deductions with much more certainty. In turn, your accountant will have the supporting documents needed to be more aggressive with your tax returns.

These 39 Tax Smart tips are strategies I use to help my clients save thousands of dollars annually on their taxes. If tailored to your unique situation, they will help you, too.

TAX CUTS AND JOBS ACT OF 2017 - THE KEY PROVISIONS

On December 22, 2017, President Donald J. Trump signed into law the Tax Cuts and Jobs Act of 2017, or the TCJA. This major legislation represented the most sweeping changes to the IRS tax code in more than 30 years.

The new law significantly reduces corporate tax rates and establishes a large new deduction for owners of pass-through entities. It provides for more modest – and temporary – reductions in individual tax rates. It also simplifies personal tax preparation by increasing the standard deduction while reducing a number of itemized deductions. Deductions for state and local taxes, and mortgage and home-equity interest, are reduced. Bonus depreciation is significantly revised, while deductions for business-related meals and other travel related costs are reduced.

Most companies and company owners will benefit from the new tax laws. The previous corporate tax rates – ranging from 15% to 35% – are replaced by a single, flat corporate rate of 21%. The corporate Alternative Minimum Tax, or AMT, is repealed, although corporations may fully use any AMT credit carryovers for tax years 2018-21. A deduction of 20% is established to owners of pass-through business entities. This is a significant new tax break available to sole proprietorships, partnerships, S corporations or LLCs considered as sole proprietorships or partnerships for tax purposes.

Bonus depreciation – where new assets, such as computers, vehicles, machinery, equipment and office furniture – can be deducted in the first year, has been doubled to 100%. This figure begins to reduce for property placed in service from 2023, ultimately falling to 20% by 2026. Some companies may not be eligible for bonus depreciation in 2018, such as larger real estate businesses (above $25 million) that deduct 100% of their business interest. In cases where a first-year bonus depreciation is not applicable, a Section 179 deduction offers similar relief; under the new legislation, the Section 179 deduction has been doubled to $1 million, although not for rental real estate.

The structure of individual tax brackets is maintained, but somewhat reduced, with the top rate falling from 39.6% to 37%. These reductions will expire in 2025. (See Tax Smart Tip #8.) At the same time, a change in the way annual inflation adjustments are calculated could edge taxpayers into higher tax brackets and therefore reduce the benefits of the various tax breaks over time.

The structure of both personal exemptions and standard deductions is largely replaced with a significantly increased standard deduction -- $12,000 for singles and separate filers, $18,000 for heads of households, and $24,000 for joint filers. At the same time, family tax credits are doubled from $1,000 to $2,000 for children under the age of 17.

Deductions for state and local taxes are reduced to $10,000 combined for state income tax and property taxes on personal residences for personal tax returns. Deductions on mortgage interest are generally allowed only on mortgage debt up to $750,000 (although remaining at $1 million for mortgages taken out before December 15, 2017). Deductions for interest on home equity debt are suspended, although this is a complex area, with a number of exceptions, and requires expert advice. None of this limits the amount of property taxes and mortgage interest which can be deducted for rental properties against rental income.

Basic Real Estate Tax Strategies

TAX SMART TIP #1
USE TAX STRATEGIES TAILORED FOR YOU

Description – Tailoring your strategies is the very essence of planning your taxes in order to minimize the amount you pay. It means using the correct strategies at the correct time and in the correct manner for your unique situation. It also means collecting and retaining the correct amount of documentation to safeguard the strategy. This is especially the case in light of the Tax Cuts and Jobs Act of 2017 which made major changes across the taxation landscape. The updated tax laws offer new opportunities for tax savings, as well as some new risks. The new laws are designed to simplify filings, but for business owners and real estate investors, they also impose a number of new and distinct requirements for documentation and careful record-keeping.

The majority of tax publications merely describe tax strategies in general without telling you, the reader, whether the strategy is actually applicable to you. This book aims to help you determine the right strategies for your situation. An effective tax strategy must also be based on up-to-date information on the most recent legislation. For this edition, several new tax strategies have been added, most chapters have been revised and updated, while some strategies which have become outdated have been omitted.

Why do I need to tailor my tax strategies as a landlord?

Because each individual's tax situation is unique, based on:

- How many properties you own
- Whether you have earned income from a job or a business
- Whether you are an active or a passive investor
- The amount of your earned income
- Your ability to qualify as an active investor or real estate professional
- Your goals and limitations

Based on these and other factors, a tax strategy that might be good for one landlord might be awful for another. In each of the subsequent tips, I will tell you why a particular strategy is valuable, when to use it and how to safeguard it.

How do I tailor my tax strategies as a landlord?

Tailoring your tax strategies basically consists of the following steps:

- Analyzing and obtaining an understanding of your situation and goals.
- Developing a strategic tax plan to minimize current and future tax liabilities.
- Preparing a tax projection which incorporates the strategic tax plan.
- Implementing the strategic tax plan including sufficient documentation to safeguard the strategy.
- Ensuring you have made sufficient tax payments to avoid a tax penalty.

Remember, tailoring of tax strategies applies both to your business entities and to your personal income taxes. The following chapters will provide you with the information you need regarding each strategy as well as a full outline of the documentation you need to safeguard each approach.

Tax $mart Tip #1

Make sure you have on your wealth team a CPA who is a real estate investor like myself. Have your CPA review your situation and tailor tax reduction strategies specifically for you. If they cannot do that, find someone else who can or visit my website at www.lanzarocpa.com to find out how to become a client.

TAX SMART TIP #2
KEEP GOOD RECORDS

Description – The Tax Cut and Jobs Act of 2017 provides additional opportunities for tax savings, especially for real estate investors and business owners. The new legislation increases the burden of record keeping and the increased savings it offers cannot be safeguarded without proper documentation. Good record keeping is therefore more important than ever.

Proper record keeping means capturing and keeping documentation on all transactions related to your business properties, including:

- Purchasing
- Selling
- Financing
- Maintaining
- Leasing
- Managing

Why do I need to keep good records?

Good record keeping is the basis for all the tax strategies discussed in this guide. A house needs a strong foundation, and the tax philosophy for your real estate business needs a strong foundation too. This means documentation. Without solid record keeping, the numbers your accountant puts on your tax returns and the strategies from this guide that you implement cannot be supported during an audit, putting you at serious risk.

What are the documentation requirements of the new legislation?

A good example of the new tax savings available under the act is the deduction for pass-through businesses. Previously, your income from a sole proprietorship was for tax purposes passed on to personally, and you paid your individual tax rate on the full amount. Under the new legislation, you may be entitled to a 20% deduction of your "qualified business income" from this business. However, any income, gain, deduction or loss from the pass-through business much be carefully documented and justified in order to calculate your deduction properly and safeguard against any future audit review.

How do I keep good records?

This question depends on the size of your business. An investor who owns one multi-family house may be able to keep track of income and expenses on column paper or an Excel® spreadsheet. If your company owns shopping centers, office buildings or multiple residential rental properties, and even has a few employees, it may need a more sophisticated accounting program like QuickBooks®. Larger businesses may choose to employ a company bookkeeper or accountant depending on their size.

Whatever your situation, here are five steps for implementing a rock-solid system for documenting business activity:

1. Choose an accounting system to track all your real estate business income and expenses. (see Tax Smart Tip #4.)

2. Decide whether you, as the investor-owner, have the necessary time and knowledge to accurately run the system. If not, hire someone to do it for you. If you do not have the knowledge, get the training necessary to be able to do it, or hire someone to do it for you.

3. Make sure your accounting system is sophisticated enough to capture all your business related activity. Too often, small real estate investors and business owners fail to do this, costing themselves in missed tax deductions.

4. Have a filing system by vendor, customer, bank, and property that allows you to find all documents related to your business at a moment's notice. If it can't do this, your system needs further work. If you don't have time to do set it up, hire someone to do it for you. The average high school student can develop a filing system for you quickly and inexpensively.

5. For larger businesses and owners of multiple properties, your system should give you the information necessary to manage your business. An accurate monthly profit and loss statement is the minimum requirement for such a system. Even better would

be a system that produces cash flow, productivity and other transactional reports.

Safeguarding and Good Record Keeping

Ignore this advice about good record keeping at your own risk. Good record keeping and having the proper documentation to prove your deductions reduces the risk of an audit by a government agency. If you do get audited, you simply have to provide this documentation to the auditor as proof that you are in compliance with the tax laws and that the return(s) being audited are correct. The primary way to do this is to have an organized, systematized system and proper documentation available to you at your fingertips. If you do not have such a system in place, and cannot produce appropriate documentation, then during an audit you could be subject to repayments, fines and other significant penalties. We will discuss accounting systems further in Tax Smart Tip #4.

Tax $mart Tip #2

Keeping good records = ability to use tax reduction strategies to minimize your taxes every year.

TAX SMART TIP #3
AVOID RECORD KEEPING NO-NO'S

Description – Record keeping no-no's are things you do not want to do as part of your record keeping system for your rental properties. These are actions that will make it more difficult for you as a landlord to capture all necessary transactions, keep proper documentation and ultimately defend yourself if audited. This section reviews each no-no, tells you why it is a bad idea and explains what actions you should take to avoid it.

Record keeping no-no's

- Commingling business and personal funds
- Paying expenses using numerous credit cards and bank accounts
- No filing system for transactional documents
- No separation of income and expenses by property
- No necessary safeguarding documentation prepared

Why it is a no-no and what is the solution?

Commingling business and personal funds

This is a no-no for several reasons:
- It can void your asset protection strategy if your properties are in business entities
- It makes it more difficult to capture all rental business-related transactions resulting in lost deductions
- It produces an audit trail that is difficult to follow and potentially can give an auditor personal information they should not have

Paying expenses using numerous credit cards and bank accounts

This is a no-no because:
- It makes it more difficult to capture all rental business-related transactions resulting in lost deductions
- It produces an audit trail that is difficult to follow and potentially can give an auditor personal information they should not have

I see this happen a lot with new investors. They pay rental business expenses from wherever they have the available funds. Sometimes, this is a necessity but it should be avoided whenever possible.

The solution is to have a separate bank account for your business where all transactions take place. All expenses are paid through this account with either checks or a debit card. Landlords requiring the use of credit cards should use one card in the name of the entity holding the property and pay the credit card bill from the same bank account used for the other transactions. In this manner, all transactions related to the business are accounted for in one bank account.

If there is not sufficient cash in your business account to pay expenses and you have the available cash in another account, you should move the funds via check or transfer into the business account and then pay the expenses. This allows for the cleanest audit trail and least opportunity for expenses to be missed.

No filing system for transactional documents

This is a no-no because you need to be able to access your transactional documents as needed to document your tax strategies and safeguard your documents in case of audit.

Setting up a filing system for your documents is a simple, low skill administrative function that can be easily outsourced to your children, an administrative assistant or a professional organizer. I recommend filing paperwork by property, type, and name.

For example, let's say you own a 4-unit property at 123 Main Street. You might have a file box or drawer in a filing cabinet labeled "123 Main Street". In that box/drawer, you have a section called "Leases" and each lease is put in a folder by tenant name. Also, you have a section called "Operating Expenses" and a folder for each vendor, contractor and service provider you use with copies of all invoices for that year in it. Use the same idea for closing statements, financing statements, insurance policies and any other important paperwork related to that property.

At the end of each year after filing your taxes, simply put that box in storage and start the next year with the same system.

No separation of income and expenses by property

This is a no-no because you want to be able to separately report income and expenses for each property. From a property management standpoint, it is also helpful to know which properties are making a profit and which are losing money. The same concept applies to cash flow – you want to know which properties generate cash and which properties are draining your cash.

The solution is to put into place an accounting system (manual or computerized) that allows you to separate income and expenses by property. For further discussion of types of accounting systems, see Tax Smart Tip #4.

No necessary safeguarding documentation prepared

The last big no-no is not implementing the necessary record keeping procedures to produce the safe-guarding documentation you will need to maximize and protect your tax deductions.

This includes:

- having the proper reports prepared for strategy implementation – for example, cost segregation studies (Tax Smart Tip #10) or abandonment studies (Tax Smart Tip #13)
- tracking time spent on your business (Tax Smart Tips #6 & #7)
- tracking miles driven for business (Tax Smart Tip #22)
- properly documenting receipts for travel, meals and entertainment (Tax Smart Tip #20)
- preparing Form 1099 for contractors and other service providers (Tax Smart Tip #23)

Record keeping requirements may appear onerous. But an awareness of what paperwork is needed and the proper filing systems to retain it will make it straightforward to fulfill the requirements. This will ensure you have the documentation you need to support the best tax strategies for your situation. Above all, it is far easier and less time consuming in the first place to establish the right documentation systems, and avoid the several no-no's, than to try to recover missing documentation or address record keeping mistakes after the fact.

Tax $mart Tip #3

Consult your CPA on how to structure your business and set up the systems necessary to avoid these no-no's.

TAX SMART TIP #4
HAVE A GOOD ACCOUNTING SYSTEM

Description – An accounting system is a means of accumulating transactional data for a business and organizing it in an efficient manner. The goal of a good accounting system is to produce the information and reports needed to run the business effectively, comply with tax reporting requirements and minimize tax liabilities. With the proliferation of smartphone apps and other tools, it is also possible to supplement your main accounting system with convenient technology to simplify your documentation and record keeping, such as tracking your hours and mileage.

What types of accounting systems are available for my business?

I am a big proponent of choosing an accounting system based on the abilities and comfort level of the person running it. I never like to force a client to use a system they don't like or are not comfortable with, because they will either do a lousy job or not do it all.

My clients basically use three types of systems:

- Paper system - summarizing transactions by category on columned paper. This is usually only efficient for landlords with a single property. The weakness of this system is that it only accounts for income and expenses. You cannot prepare a balance sheet from this information.
- Computer spreadsheet system - summarizing transactions by category using a spreadsheet program like Microsoft Excel®. This is basically a computerized version of the paper system that allows for the use of computer functions to add, subtract, sort and perform other tasks. This is usually only effective for landlords with a maximum of three properties. Again, the weakness of this system is that it only accounts for income and expenses. You cannot prepare a balance sheet from this information.
- Computer accounting software - computer software that uses a double entry accounting system to account for transactions and includes account categories for assets, liabilities and equity accounts in addition to income and expense account categories. Typically,

this type of software allows you to keep a running balance on your checking account, tells you which tenants owe you money, as well as which vendors you owe money to, and produces multiple reports that include a balance sheet and profit and loss statement. QuickBooks® is the most popular brand of this type of accounting software currently in use for rental property businesses. This type of system can be used for any size business from a single property to multiple properties in a single entity. The primary weakness of this type of system is that it may be too complicated for someone with limited accounting knowledge to run and may require professional accounting assistance.

In short, a good accounting system:

- Accounts for all transactions of a rental business
- Provides an audit trail for the landlord
- Makes preparing reports needed for management, compliance and tax minimization easy
- Makes it less expensive to have your taxes prepared
- Makes it easier to document and protect your tax deductions

Can smartphone apps help?

There are an increasing number of smartphone apps available to help you track your time and expenses and streamline the process of recording keeping. Some can even feed directly into your accounting system and help make running your business a lot easier.

Here are some of the main types of apps you might want to investigate and adopt:

- Timesheet and time management – there are a number of effective apps for tracking your own time. Once you have downloaded an app and set it up according to your tasks, you can easily "tap in and out" to indicate, for example, which specific property you are spending your time on. The data is only as good as you make it. If you use consistently, these apps will allow you to create reports to show exactly how you have spent your time. This can be very useful information if you are ever audited.
- Mileage tracking – It can be cumbersome to keep track of your mileage, especially if you are operating multiple properties. Mileage tracking apps perform the task for you automatically as

you drive. The app will produce a report indicating the mileage you have traveled for business purposes. This will help ensure that you distinguish between business and personal driving, which is essential for meeting IRS standards.

- Expenses and receipt scanning – it can be especially challenging to finish the day, week or even month with a pile of receipts on your desk. This makes it difficult to remember which expenses were business related and for which property. It is a good habit to write a note on every receipt you get stating the business purpose, expense category and property address. Expense apps enable you to scan receipts and immediately allocate them to business activities. Once the receipts are scanned, the app can produce a full report on your expenses with an image of the documentation incorporated, all customizable to your requirements. These apps can be great time savers and can really complement your accounting system.

Tax $mart Tip #4

The most current version of QuickBooks Pro will work well for landlords. Consult a CPA to set up your company file properly which is the key to getting off to a good start with QuickBooks.

TAX SMART TIP #5
AVOID BEING A PASSIVE INVESTOR

Description – Active investors enjoy increased tax advantages. Being a passive investor is a classification that means not being able to deduct rental losses against other income on your tax return. The Tax Cuts and Jobs Act of 2017 did not change these rules.

How can I tell if I am a passive investor?

You are a passive real estate investor if:

- You own less than 10% of a property
- You have no substantial involvement in the management of the property
- You have a property manager managing the property; this applies even if you perform some tasks for the property
- You qualify as an active investor but your adjusted gross income from other sources is too high to deduct rental losses (Tax Smart Tip #6)

Why is classification as a passive investor bad?

Your classification as either passive or active determines your ability to deduct rental losses against your other income. One of the big advantages of owning rental properties is that you can shelter the cash flow produced by the property using the depreciation deduction to offset the taxable income. This puts cash in your pocket that you don't have to pay taxes on in the year you get it!

What happens if I am a passive investor?

If you are a passive investor:

- You can only deduct rental losses against other passive investment income
- Losses not deducted in the current year are carried over to the next year
- All losses carried over to future years are deductible in the year the property is sold

Passive income example

Richard and John own a building that they lease to a tenant. Each of them owns 50% of the property. However, John does all of the work related to the management of the property which amounts to about 400 hours per year. The property makes about $50,000 a year of cash flow but shows a tax loss of $10,000 a year because of depreciation.

Result: Richard is considered a passive investor and can only deduct his portion of the loss on this building if he has other passive income. If he does not, the loss will be carried over every year on his tax return until he either has passive income to offset or the property is sold.

How do I get around being a passive investor?

Qualify as either an active investor or a real estate professional (Tax Smart Tips #6 and #7)

TAX SMART TIP #6
BE AN ACTIVE INVESTOR

Description – Being an active investor offers significant tax advantages. Classification as an active investor means that you can deduct up to $25,000 of rental losses annually against other income, subject to certain limitations.

How can I tell if I am an active investor?

You are an active real estate investor if:

- You own more than 10% of a property, and
- You have substantial involvement in the management of the property

Why is this important?

Your classification as either passive or active determines your ability to deduct rental losses against your other income and avoid passive loss limitations (Tax Smart Tip #5). One of the big advantages of owning rental properties is that you can shelter cash flow by using the depreciation deduction to offset the net rental income. As an active investor, you can also use up to $25,000 of rental losses to offset income from wages, businesses and other sources.

How does that work?

If you are an active investor:

- You can deduct up to $25,000 per year of rental losses against income from non-passive sources such as wages or self-employment income
- The $25,000 of allowable losses can be phased out for taxpayers whose adjusted gross income exceeds $100,000 per year and is completely phased out at $150,000 per year of adjusted gross income
- Allowable losses or losses exceeding $25,000 per year that are not deducted in the current year are carried over to the next year

Note that these rules are largely unchanged by the Tax Cuts and Jobs Act of 2017. However, the new tax law does offer additional tax planning opportunities to reduce income below $150,000. Remaining below this threshold, if possible, allows active investors to deduct up to $25,000 of rental losses against income.

To establish that you are and remain an active investor, time management apps for your smartphone can be a great help in monitoring and documenting the hours you spend on your real estate investment business. Remember that is it not enough to own the property (more than 10%), you also have to spend a substantial amount of time in managing it. A time management app can track your hours and produce reports so that you can document this.

Here are some examples using the same scenario from Tax Smart Tip #5:

Example #1

Richard and John own a building that they lease to a tenant. Each of them owns 50% of the property. However, John does all of the work related to the management of the property which amounts to about 400 hours per year. The property makes about $50,000 a year of cash flow but shows a tax loss of $10,000 a year because of depreciation.

Result: John is considered an active investor and will be able to deduct his $5,000 loss ($10,000 x 50% ownership) against his non-passive income if his adjusted gross income is less than $100,000 that year.

Example #2

Let's use the same facts as example #1 except that both Richard and John share equally in the management of the rental property and no management company is used.

Result: Both Richard and John are considered active investors and can deduct their respective $5,000 losses ($10,000 x 50% ownership) against their non-passive income if their adjusted gross income is less than $100,000 that year.

As you can see, it makes a huge difference from a tax standpoint if you actively manage your properties assuming you make less than $150,000 of adjusted gross income per year (the phase out limit). If you make more than $150,000 of adjusted gross income per year, then you may be better off leaving the management of your properties to a property manager, as you get no real tax benefit from the work.

Tax Planning Opportunity

In circumstances where an individual landlord's adjusted gross income for the year exceeds $150,000 and they have rental losses that could be deducted, various types of tax planning can allow the investor to lower their adjusted gross income below the $150,000 limit in order to take losses. For a discussion of these strategies, see Tax Smart Tip #29

How do I maintain proper documentation of my real estate hours to prove I am an active investor?

Landlord investors should keep time logs by property summarizing the hours spent performing various tasks related to the management of each rental property. This can be done by hand, or by smartphone apps, which can be highly useful.

Tax $mart Tip #6

Qualifying as an active investor has huge tax advantages. You must keep records of the time you spend managing your properties which can be done by hand, on a computer spreadsheet or using a time tracking app on your smart phone.

TAX SMART TIP #7
QUALIFY AS A REAL ESTATE PROFESSIONAL

Description – An individual who qualifies as a real estate professional can take unlimited losses from rental properties against their earned income. This offers significant potential tax advantages.

How can I tell if I qualify as a real estate professional?

You qualify as a real estate professional if you meet all of the following criteria:

- You are involved in the operations of the rental activity on a regular, continuous and substantial basis.
- At least 50% of your personal services during the tax year are performed in real property trades or in a business in which you materially participate.
- You spend more than 750 hours of service during the tax year in real property trades or businesses in which you materially participate.
- You are in a real property trade or business such as real estate development, redevelopment, construction, reconstruction, acquisition, conversion, rental, operations, management, leasing or brokerage.

Why is this important?

Your classification as a real estate professional determines your ability to deduct rental losses against your other income and avoid passive loss limitations and active investor income limitations (Tax Smart Tip #5 & #6). One of the big advantages of owning rental properties is that you can shelter cash flow by using the depreciation deduction to offset the net rental income. As a real estate professional, you can use unlimited rental losses to offset income from wages, businesses, and other sources.

How does this work?

If you are a real estate professional:

- You can deduct all losses incurred from real estate rentals against income from non-passive sources like wages and business income.

- The earned income from your real estate businesses (not rental income) may be subject to self-employment tax.

Here are some examples:

Example #1

John is a real estate broker who owns several buildings which he leases to tenants. John meets all of the criteria to be classified as a real estate professional. John's properties show a tax loss of $30,000 a year because of depreciation. John has earned income as a real estate broker of $200,000.

Result: John may deduct all of his $30,000 loss against his $200,000 of earned income because he qualifies as a real estate professional. This means John only pays income taxes on $170,000 of income. John is not subject to passive loss rules, the active investor rental loss limitation of $25,000, or the $150,000 adjusted gross income limitation that passive and active investors are subject to.

Example #2

Let's use the same facts as example #1 except that John spends 800 hours as a real estate broker and property manager, but also spends 1,000 hours working in a printing business.

Result: John does not qualify as a real estate professional because he spends over 50% of his time in a non-real estate business (printing). As a result, John is considered an active investor. John's $200,000 of broker income exceeds the income limitation to take deductions as an active investor ($150,000 of adjusted gross income). John cannot deduct any of his rental losses against his income because he does not qualify as a real estate professional.

How do I maintain proper documentation of my hours to prove I am a real estate professional?

Landlord investors should keep time logs by property summarizing the hours spent performing various tasks related to the management of the rental property. In addition, to qualify as a real estate professional, you must also document the hours you spend in your real estate trade or businesses and the hours you spend in any business not related to real estate. You can do this by keeping time logs on a spreadsheet. You can also keep records by hand and enter them into your computer regularly. A very efficient solution is to utilize a smartphone timesheet or time management app. This allow you, with a simple touch of the screen, to toggle between different tasks so that you can easily track your hours during the day, and print out full reports on a weekly, monthly, quarterly or annual basis as you need.

Tax $mart Tip #7

Landlords/investors should keep time logs by property summarizing the hours spent performing various tasks related to the management of their rental properties. In addition, to qualify as a real estate professional, you must also document the hours you spend in your real estate trade or business, and the hours you spend in any business not related to real estate.

TAX SMART TIP #8
AVOID OVERPAYING YOUR ESTIMATED TAXES

Description – A key part of cash and tax management is ensuring that you pay the appropriate amount of estimated taxes based on your current estimates of your income without paying too much money to the IRS or state government. The Tax Cuts and Jobs Act of 2017 did not change the rules on making estimated payments. It did, however, reduce individual tax rates, so depending on your income level, your personal tax liability may be reduced.

Why is this important?

Estimated tax payments are used to pay taxes on income that is not subject to tax withholding. If you do not pay taxes on your income from sources not subject to tax withholding, you will face penalties for underpayment. Also, if you do not pay your estimated taxes by the proper due date, you may be subject to penalties for late payment. However, if you overpay your estimated taxes, you are giving the government an interest-free loan and tying up cash flow that can be used for investing in additional properties, managing your properties or paying personal expenses.

How have rates changed?

Under the new legislation, the seven primary income brackets are maintained, but most of the rates are reduced beginning in 2018 and will expire in 2025. There are also adjustments in the income ranges for several of the brackets. A full table of the revised tax brackets for individuals, married couples and heads of households is provided in the appendix. The main changes for individuals from 2017 to 2018 are summarized below:

As you can see, 5 of the 7 income brackets has a rate reduction for tax years 2018 to 2025 ranging from 1% to 4% with an average rate reduction of about 2% in total.

Individual Tax Rates	Individual Tax Rates
2017	2018 - 2025
10.0%	10.0%
15.0%	12.0%
25.0%	22.0%
28.0%	24.0%
33.0%	32.0%
35.0%	35.0%
39.6%	37.0%

What types of income are subject to estimated tax payments?

You may be required to make estimated tax payments on your income from:

- A sole proprietorship, LLC or S corporation
- Interest and dividends
- Net rental income
- Capital gains from sales of property and other investments
- Alimony or other sources of income

Who needs to make estimated payments?

You have to make estimated tax payments if you expect to owe tax of $1,000 or more when you file your personal income taxes. Also, you have to make estimated payments if you had a tax liability for the prior year and you anticipate your income will be equal to or higher than your prior year's income.

How do I know how much to pay in estimated taxes?

Here is where good record keeping and having a good accounting system are invaluable. If you have these in place, it is much easier to project how much income you will be reporting when you file your personal income taxes.

Paying your estimated taxes is based on your tax planning (Tax Smart Tip #9). As part of tax planning, I prepare a tax projection for a client several times a year in advance of the due date of an estimated payment. As a result, we are able to make the exact estimated payment for the income earned up to the due date of the estimated payment. In addition, we avoid overpaying our taxes. This keeps cash available for investing and personal use, and we do not give the government an interest-free loan. All of this is well-documented, justified and properly safeguarded.

When are estimated tax payments due?

Estimated tax payments are due on the following dates for income earned in the following periods:

- April 15th for income earned from January to March
- June 15th for income earned from April to May
- September 15th for income earned from June to August
- January 15th of the following year for income earned from September to December

How do I avoid underpayment penalties?

If you did not pay enough tax throughout the year, either through withholding or by making estimated tax payments, you may have to pay a penalty for underpayment of estimated tax.

You can avoid this penalty if you:

- Owe less than $1,000 in tax after subtracting your withholding and credits on your annual tax return
- Pay at least 90% of the tax owed for your current year's personal income tax return, or
- Pay 100% of the tax shown on your personal income tax return for the prior year, if smaller than the 90% of tax owed for your current year's personal income tax return.

Note: If your adjusted gross income is over $150,000 on your prior year's personal income tax return, you must pay 110% of the tax shown on that return as estimated payments for the current year to penalty proof yourself.

Tax $mart Tip #8

Meet with your CPA every quarter to calculate the amount of estimated payments due. This will keep you from overpaying or underpaying your taxes every year.

TAX SMART TIP #9
DO TAX PLANNING ANNUALLY

Description – Tax planning is the process of developing a tailored, strategic plan to minimize the amount of income taxes that must be paid on your income annually. The Tax Cuts and Jobs Act of 2017 offers a number of new ways to reduce the amount of income tax owed annually. However, it is vital for any real estate investor serious about tax minimization to undertake a fresh and thorough planning process in order to lower their taxes.

Why is this important?

One of the biggest mistakes made by real estate landlords is waiting until it is too late to assess the tax impact of their rental income and real estate purchase and sale transactions. If you do not do annual tax planning, you are missing out on strategies that must be implemented prior to year-end in order to be effective. In essence, you are voluntarily overpaying your income taxes.

This is especially important in light of the new legislation, which offers opportunities for reducing your taxes. A sound tax plan needs to take into consideration how to maximize depreciation, the new Section 199 tax deduction, assess availability of tax credits and maximize opportunities to defer taxes with retirement plan contributions and Section 1031 exchanges of sales of properties.

That sounds stupid! Why would anyone not do annual tax planning?

There are several reasons for this:

- The new tax laws are complicated and require expert advice to maximize tax planning.
- Landlords often fear an IRS audit if they aggressively pursue tax savings.
- Landlords often do not think about their taxes until the filing deadline is imminent.

However, real estate landlords only need to remember that the IRS only requires you to pay the amount of tax you owe under the law, and NOT A PENNY MORE! In numerous tax court cases, judges have noted that it is the taxpayer's right and obligation to reduce their taxes to the minimum amount due as long as they comply with the tax code.

What factors are involved in tax planning?

There are several factors to consider when developing a tailored strategic tax plan for a real estate investor's unique situation. Tax strategies that provide the most benefit should take into account the following:

- What specific changes in the new legislation impact your unique tax situation?
- How does the timing of a transaction impact the situation?
- What options are available to minimize your taxable income?
- Can you defer taxable income or tax payments without incurring a penalty?
- What is your marginal tax rate and how does a given transaction affect that rate?
- Can you offset high income with high expenses?
- What is the effect of long term versus short term holding periods?

What is involved in preparing a strategic tax plan?

While each taxpayer's situation is unique, strategic tax planning basically consists of the following steps (See Tax Smart Tip #1):

- Analyzing and obtaining an understanding of the taxpayer's situation and goals.
- Developing a strategic tax plan to minimize current and future tax liabilities in light of current legislation.
- Preparing a tax projection which incorporates the strategic tax plan.
- Implementing the strategic tax plan.
- Ensuring that the taxpayer has made sufficient tax payments to avoid a tax penalty.

A good example of the new opportunity for tax reduction in the new legislation is the Section 199 deduction for pass-through businesses, such as a sole proprietorship or partnership. Previously, income from a pass-through business was considered for tax purposes as direct income for the owner(s) of the business, and therefore fully subject to applicable income tax rates. Under the new legislation, a 20% deduction on an owner's qualified

31

business income is available. This is a huge benefit, but appropriate tax planning will ensure that the right steps are taking to account for the income properly and calculate and safeguard the full deduction amount.

Tax $mart Tip #9

You should implement strategic tax planning annually in order to reduce the amount of taxes you pay every year. Contact me at ted@lanzarocpa.com if you would like me to develop a strategic tax plan to save you thousands of dollars every year.

Tax Strategies
When Buying Real Estate

TAX SMART TIP #10
SEGREGATE COSTS TO ACCELERATE DEPRECIATION

Description – A cost segregation study is an engineering-based study that allows a commercial building owner, whether residential or non-residential, to accelerate a substantial amount of the depreciation deductions by identifying construction or acquisition costs that can be allocated to a shorter recovery period.

Why is a cost segregation study an important tax strategy?

Cost segregation studies offer a tremendous opportunity to increase cash flow and defer tax payments until later years. It is a great tool to accelerate the return on capital from your investment in property. This valuable strategy for reducing tax payments and protecting cash flow did not change with the enactment of the Tax Cuts and Jobs Act of 2017. However, new limits on bonus depreciation and new bonus depreciation categories mean that the potential benefits of cost segregation have become even more important. (See Tax Smart Tips #11 & #12 for additional information)

How does a cost segregation study work?

The basic idea is to move building costs that would ordinarily be depreciated over 27.5 or 39 years to depreciation over 5, 7, or 15 years using an IRS approved, engineering-based study as proof that the cost should be depreciated over a shorter life.

What are the steps to a cost segregation study?

There are three main steps used by engineers to complete the cost segregation study:

- Make an initial land to building cost allocation (see Tax Smart Tip #11).
- Analyze land improvement costs, for example, landscaping, fencing or paving.
- Analyze building costs by breaking them into component parts

of the building and applying the correct depreciable useful life to them.

What are the results of a cost segregation study?

- Land improvements are depreciated over 15 years as opposed to not being depreciated or being depreciated over much longer period – as a rule, 27.5 years for residential buildings and 39 years for commercial buildings.
- Tangible personal property separated from building costs are depreciated from 5 to 7 years as opposed to the usual 27.5 or 39 year terms.

When should a cost segregation study be used?

Cost segregation should be considered as an appropriate tax strategy when one or more of the following apply:

- The owner(s) of the property are active investors or real estate professionals.
- The owner(s) have a lot of real estate rental income that could be offset with accelerated depreciation.
- The property is expected to be held longer than 3 years as a rental proper

Let's look at some examples where a cost segregation study is appropriate:

Initial Construction

Generally speaking, this is the easiest type of study to perform because the engineers get involved right from the beginning and have access to the architectural drawings and building invoices. Let's use an actual example of a 4 story office building completed at a total construction cost of $9.6 million. Without the help of an expert CPA and engineer, the building owner would be depreciating the $9.6 million cost over 39 years. With a cost segregation study, the engineers examine all the construction invoices and design documents. They do an on-site study to identify, measure, quantify and photograph the existence of all the assets within the building that qualify for accelerated depreciation.

End Result: By performing the study, the engineers are able to allocate

$1.95 million, or 20% of the assets, to shorter recovery periods, while also saving the property owner more than $427,000 in income taxes!

Property Acquisition

A cost segregation study can also be performed when a commercial property owner acquires a property. Generally speaking, there are two types of these studies:

- Contemporaneous studies that are performed around the period of acquisition
- "Look-back" studies that are performed after the fact, even if the acquisition or construction was several years ago

For example, a local regional mall was purchased by a real estate investment company. The 2 story mall was purchased for $25.6 million. Without a cost segregation study, the acquisition cost allocated to the building (most likely about 80%) would be depreciated over 39 years. The remaining land cost (20%) would not be depreciated.

Upon acquiring the property, the new owners had an engineering based cost segregation study performed. Using whatever initial construction data that was available from the prior owner (sometimes there is no information available) and by performing a detailed on-site evaluation and identification process including photographing all the assets, the engineers were able to determine which assets were eligible for accelerated depreciation.

End Result: A total of $9.8 million of assets (38% of the total cost) was determined to qualify for either 5 year or 15 year depreciation resulting in a net present value tax savings of $1.5 million over the first 10 years of the property ownership and $250,000 of tax savings in the first year.

When performing a look-back study, often none of the construction information is available. A retrospective study typically relies on the engineer's on-site evaluation and identification of qualified assets. However, a property owner doing an after-the-fact review can often receive a terrific amount of tax savings in the first year because according to Internal Revenue Code Section 418(a), the property owner is allowed is make an adjustment to catch up on depreciation. The catch up is equal to the difference between what was depreciated and what could have been depreciated had a cost segregation study been performed on day one.

Let's look at another example:

A small suburban office building was purchased by its owners several years ago at a cost of $10 million. At this time, the owner's accountant began depreciating the property over 39 years. Recently, a cost segregation study was performed. The study identified $800,000 of assets that could be reallocated to a 5 year recovery period.

Result: Last year, the property owner was allowed a catch up on more than $680,000 of depreciation which resulted in a $238,000 tax savings under Internal Revenue Code Section 481(a).

Leasehold Improvements

Both tenants and landlords can take advantage of a cost segregation study when they are required to invest in fitting out a space. A typical cost segregation study can re-allocate over 30% of leasehold improvements, normally depreciated over 39 years, to 5 and 7 year recovery periods.

An example of this occurred when a high-end restaurant, bar and grill leased and built out its space in a suburban shopping mall. The restaurant owners spent more than $1.4 million on the custom fit-out of the restaurant space. A cost segregation study was performed by a team that reviewed the construction documents and conducted an on-site evaluation of the construction. Again, assets were identified and photographed and the costs of the identified assets were quantified.

Result: From this study, $924,000 of assets were re-allocated (65.2%) to shorter recovery periods resulting in more than $236,000 in net present value tax savings over 10 years and $17,000 of tax savings in the first year.

What kind of investment properties can benefit from using cost segregation?

Any of the following types of properties with a cost basis exceeding $750,000 can benefit from a cost segregation study:

- office buildings
- shopping malls
- strip shopping centers
- apartment buildings
- large leasehold fit-outs

- auto dealerships
- free standing out-parcel buildings used for large retail stores or chain fast food restaurants
- hotels and resorts
- distribution warehouses
- manufacturing facilities
- industrial buildings
- self-storage buildings

How do I safeguard this strategy?

The best approach is to work with a reputable CPA and a tax engineering firm to prepare a written report with asset detail supporting the reclassification of the useful lives of the building components. The CPA uses the report to prepare the building depreciation schedule on the tax return in order to take the tax deductions that result in significant tax savings

Tax $mart Tip #10

Cost Segregation Studies are an incredible tool for tax savings on income producing properties if you are an active investor or real estate professional.

TAX SMART TIP #11
REDUCE THE COST BASIS ALLOCATED TO LAND

Description – The original purchase price of an income producing property must be broken down between the portion that is attributable to depreciable building and land improvements, and the portion attributed to the land which is not depreciable. The rules on this have not been changed under the new Tax Cuts and Jobs Act of 2017.

Why is this important?

Since land cost is not depreciable, the more cost basis allocated to the cost of the land purchased, the less depreciation deduction the property owner will receive over the life of the property.

Typically, an average accountant will use the "80/20" rule which is really not a rule at all. It is more of a shortcut used by tax preparers to assign a value to the cost basis of a property purchased. The accountant simply allocates 80% of the original purchase price to the building and 20% to the land. This shortcut will cost you money as an investor.

Who should use this strategy?

Property owners should use this strategy every time they purchase an income producing property. There is simply no other alternative that makes sense to maximize your depreciation deduction. On smaller properties where formal cost segregation studies are not cost effective, the property owner should work with their CPA and a property appraiser to break out the obvious components that will apply to step #1 and #2 of the following cost allocation process.

What is the most tax advantageous way of determining land cost basis?

The most tax advantageous way of determining the land cost basis of an income producing property is to implement the following steps, breaking down the total property cost into four components:

1.   Tangible personal property - This is basically all the components of the building that can be depreciated over 5 to 7 years and includes

items which can be moved such as furniture, tools, machinery and signs.

2. Land Improvements - These are things like landscaping, driveways, sidewalks, fences and other items that can be depreciated over 15 years.

3. Building - This is the rest of the building that will be depreciated over 27.5 years (residential) or 39 years (commercial). It is important to remember that the component parts of the building structure should be broken down by component in order to facilitate writing off items when they are abandoned during renovation of the property. (See Tax Smart Tip #13.)

4. The remaining balance is allocated to the land and is not depreciated.

How do I break out the various components to determine land cost basis?

Making these determinations is not difficult, and the property owner is usually the best person to list the various components. You basically just need to make a detailed list, estimate the values and calculate the totals, and provide this with appropriate documentation such as photographs to your CPA.

Tangible personal property will generally be anything that can be detached and removed in the property. Examples are appliances, sinks, lighting, shelving and cabinets. A full list of these items is located in the appendix of the book. These are 5 or 7 year assets, and the value can be determined by checking their price on a common website for home improvement such as Lowe's or Home Depot. (Print these off for documentation.) New items should be valued using a percentage of the price found – new or excellent condition items at 90%, good condition items at 60%, average condition items at 40% and poor condition items at 20%. It is also prudent to be conservative with your estimates and apply judgement and common sense to the process.

Land improvements are 15 year items. These are found outside the building on the property and may including fences, sidewalks, drains, sprinklers, lighting and retaining walls. A full list of these items is located in the appendix of the book. They can be listed and valued in the same way, and discounted on the same basis according to their condition. Remember also to include the value of wiring or plumbing. For some items, you will need to measure them, for example, to determine the length of fencing or the square footage of a driveway.

How do I safeguard the allocation of cost basis to land?

On larger properties, a cost segregation study should be performed. This engineering based study provides a report that is virtually indisputable by the IRS if it prepared by a reputable engineering firm. On smaller properties, the property owner should engage a CPA and property appraiser to work together to look for obvious components that will apply - photograph them, list them and have an appraiser value them as part of the safeguarding documentation.

Tax $mart Tip #11

Avoid using the 80/20 rule to allocate the cost basis of the rental properties you buy, and hire a real estate specific CPA who knows how to break out the components of your building to maximize depreciation.

TAX SMART TIP #12
USE SECTION 179 AND BONUS DEPRECIATION

Description – Section 179 of the Internal Revenue Tax Code allows you to fully depreciate assets with useful lives of 5 to 15 years in the first year they are placed into service. Bonus depreciation allows you to depreciate 100% of the cost of an asset with a useful life of 5 to 15 years in the first year before you calculate the regular depreciation on the asset. Provisions and limits for both of these forms of depreciation have been substantially revised under the Tax Cuts and Jobs Act of 2017, allowing for increased tax savings.

Why is this important?

Depreciation is what makes real estate a great tax shelter for cash flow. Depreciation is an allocation of the cost basis of a building and its components over the useful life of the components. (See Tax Smart Tip #10 & #11.) You can deduct depreciation against the net income of a property even though you have not actually paid it out in cash. This means you pay less income tax on the cash flow your property produces. The new rules and limitations under the recent tax law changes for both Section 179 and bonus depreciation underline the importance of depreciation for any serious tax strategy.

How does depreciation shelter cash flow?

Depreciation of a building is an expense that is taken against the net income of a property, which creates less taxable income even though you get to keep the money.

An example:

John purchases a residential apartment building for $1,000,000. The building generates net cash flow of $120,000 per year. Depreciation calculated based on the cost of the building amounts to $40,000 per year.

John earns actual cash in hand of $120,000 but only pays income tax on $80,000 (that is, the income less the depreciation amount). John has sheltered $40,000 of cash flow using depreciation.

How does Section 179 depreciation work?

Section 179 allows you to expense the full cost basis of assets with 5 to 15 year useful lives in the first year they are placed into service, subject to certain limitations, which have been increased, as follows:

- Under the new legislation, Section 179 depreciation is allowable on qualifying assets up to $1,000,000, doubled from the 2017 limit.
- The new legislation expands the definition of eligible property that can be depreciated under Section 179 so that it now includes improvements to nonresidential real estate such as roofs, fire alarms, security systems and heating/cooling equipment.
- The new legislation retains the previous stipulation that Section 179 depreciation can only be used to offset income to break even and cannot be used to create a loss.

You take Section 179 depreciation on fixed assets by making an election to do so in the year you place the assets in service.

An example:

John purchased the building he runs his business from in 2018 for $1,000,000. A cost segregation study (see Tax Smart Tip #10) determined that $100,000 of the cost of the building relates to 5 year property used in his business. John will have net income of $120,000 in 2018 before depreciation. John can take Section 179 depreciation and fully depreciate the $100,000 of 5 year cost against his income in 2018. By doing so, John will only pay income taxes on $20,000 ($120,000 of net income less $100,000 of Section 179 depreciation).

How does bonus depreciation work?

Bonus depreciation has also been significantly improved under the Tax Cuts and Jobs Act of 2017. This form of depreciation now allows you to expense fully 100% of the initial cost basis of assets with 5 to 15 year useful lives in the first year they are placed into service. This is double the 2017 limit for qualifying assets. Bonus depreciation has also been expanded so that it now applies to both used as well as new qualifying property or assets.

Unlike Section 179 depreciation, there are no limitations to how much bonus depreciation you can take in a year. The new 100% bonus depreciation

43

provisions apply for assets placed into service between September 28, 2017 and December 31, 2022.

Following that timeframe, allowable bonus depreciation is scheduled to be reduced by 20% per year – that is, decreasing to 80% of first year cost for most property placed in service in 2023 and reaching 20% in 2026.

You take bonus depreciation on fixed assets by making an election to do so in the year you place the assets in service.

An example:

John purchased his apartment building in 2018 for $1,000,000. A cost segregation study (see Tax Smart Tip #10) determined that $100,000 of the cost of the building relates to 5 year property. John has net income of $40,000 in 2018 before depreciation. John can take 100% bonus depreciation of $100,000 against his income in 2018. By doing so, John creates a loss of $70,000 ($40,000 of net income less $110,000 of bonus depreciation) that can be used to offset his other rental income and possibly his ordinary income if he is an active investor or real estate professional (See Tax Smart Tips #6 and #7)

Note that unlike Section 179 depreciation, bonus depreciation can be used to create a rental loss on a property.

When do I use this strategy?

You use this strategy in conjunction with a cost segregation study (See Tax Smart Tip #10) every time you purchase a building or make improvements to an income producing property.

How do I safeguard my depreciation deductions when using this strategy?

A cost segregation study done by a licensed tax engineering firm virtually guarantees that you will be able to break out the components of a building that qualify as 5 to 15 year useful life assets. Once that is accomplished, depreciation is just a mathematical calculation. In addition, you must make the proper elections on your tax return to take Section 179 or bonus depreciation. You should also always keep your purchase closing statements and invoices for all repair or renovation work done on your property.

Tax $mart Tip #12

Maximizing depreciation deductions means more cash in your pocket and less tax paid to the government. Your ability to use this strategy is based on your CPA's understanding of how to break down the cost basis of a building into its depreciable components. Contact me at ted@lanzarocpa.com if you would like me to perform this service for you.

TAX SMART TIP #13
TAKE ORDINARY LOSSES ON ABANDONED ASSETS

Description – Building components removed during the renovation of an income producing property can be written off at their net cost basis to create an ordinary loss not subject to passive activity rules. The new Tax Cuts and Jobs Act of 2017 did not change these rules.

Why is this important?

An investor who purchases an income producing property requiring renovation has a huge opportunity to break out the individual building components (units of property) and then write off those components disposed of during renovation.

What is a unit of property?

A unit of property refers to the various systems that make up a building. These can be defined as:

- Heating, ventilation and air conditioning systems
- Plumbing systems
- Electrical systems
- All escalators
- All elevators
- Fire protection and alarm systems
- Security systems for protection of building
- Gas distribution systems
- The remaining building structure that includes walls, windows, doors, floors, roof and concrete

When should I use this strategy?

This strategy is used primarily when demolishing and renovating a building that is used for business or income producing purposes.

An example:

John paid $3,000,000 to purchase a 100 unit apartment building that requires renovation to improve the dwellings and attract new tenants.

Each apartment consists of 2 bedroom and 1 bathroom, with a living room and a kitchen.

Each unit needs a new kitchen and bathroom. The plan is to gut the existing kitchens and bathrooms and replace them with newly installed components - cabinets, sinks, appliances, shower, etc.

Here is how it would work:

- First, an allocation of the original purchase price of $3,000,000 is made to each old kitchen and bathroom. For example, let's assume we allocate $2,000 of the purchase price to each kitchen and $1,000 of the purchase price to each bathroom.
- Prior to renovation, we take photographs and document the items in the old kitchens and bathrooms that will be disposed of.
- We do the renovation. Upon completion, we have disposed of $200,000 of kitchens ($2000 x 100) and $100,000 of bathrooms ($1,000 x 100).

Result: John gets to write off the $300,000 from the original cost basis of the property as an ordinary loss on his tax return and he adds the cost of the new kitchens and bathrooms to the cost basis of the property.

How do you implement and safeguard this deduction?

The IRS requires an abandonment study to be performed by a tax engineering firm to prepare a report to document the deduction.

Tax $mart Tip #13

Assets abandoned during the renovation of an income producing property can result in a huge tax benefit. If you are purchasing an income producing property that you will be renovating, then this strategy can result in huge tax savings.

TAX SMART TIP #14
USE TAX PLANNING WHEN CONSTRUCTING A BUILDING

Description -- Use of tax planning to identify tax benefits related to new and planned construction during the design and construction phases. The Tax Cuts and Jobs Act of 2017 did not change the rules related to this but did increase the Section 179 and bonus depreciation limits discussed earlier (Tax Smart Tip #12)

Why is this important?

Taking a proactive approach to maximizing tax benefits as part of the design and construction of a building can save hundreds of thousands of dollars, if not millions, to the owner of the building.

Who should use this strategy?

Any building owner or business owner who is designing and building a new building or redeveloping an old building where the owner has business and/or rental income which can be offset by the tax deductions created by the construction of the new building.

What are the benefits of using this strategy?

The primary benefit of using this strategy is to identify opportunities to accelerate depreciation deductions by analyzing, documenting, and constructing in a manner that optimizes building components being categorized as personal property (5 to 15 years depreciation life) instead of real property (27.5 to 39 year depreciation life).

Construction components under consideration for optimizing include:

- Interior walls and partitions
- Ceilings
- Flooring
- Chair rails, moldings and other wall finishes
- Heating and cooling systems
- Plumbing systems
- Electrical systems

- Items attached to the building such as decks and canopies
- Site improvements like parking lots, landscaping and walkways

Is there additional tax or business benefits to using this strategy?

Yes, there are numerous other benefits to using this strategy that can save the building owner money including –

- Taking advantage of federal energy efficiency incentives
- Taking advantage of state and local energy rebates and incentives
- Obtaining LEED commissioning
- Obtaining proper liability insurance coverage

How do I implement and safeguard the deductions I get from using this strategy?

You implement this strategy by consulting with and engaging a real estate CPA and tax engineering firm during the design and construction of the building to work in coordination with the architect, engineer, and general contractor constructing the building. The CPA and engineering firm document and provide a report of the implementation of the strategy during the construction phase which safeguards the deductions you will get.

Tax $mart Tip #14

Use construction tax planning any time you are building or renovating a large building. Consult a real estate CPA and tax engineering firm during the design and construction of the building to work in coordination with the architect, engineer and general contractor when constructing the building.

49

TAX SMART TIP #15
GET A TAX CREDIT FOR FIXING UP OLDER OR HISTORIC BUILDINGS

Description -- Obtaining a tax credit for making improvements to older or historic buildings that offset income tax dollar for dollar. The "Tax Cuts and Jobs Act of 2017" repealed a rehabilitation credit equal to 10% of the cost of renovating a non- historic building built before 1936 for use in operating a trade or business or for the production of rental income. This credit is not longer available for tax years 2018 and beyond.

Why is this important?

This strategy can be used to obtain a tax credit that offsets tax liabilities dollar for dollar.

Who should use this strategy?

Any building owner or business owner who is renovating or redeveloping a historic building for income producing purposes. The building must be listed in the National Register or be located in a registered district that is certified by the US Secretary of the Interior.

What are the benefits of using this strategy?

The IRS wants to create an incentive for investors and business owners to preserve older buildings of historic significance. They offer tax credits to taxpayers who either directly rehabilitate or redevelop a historic building or invest in the rehabilitation of a historic building.

The historic that credit that remains available as part of the Tax Cuts and Jobs Act of 2017 is a rehabilitation credit equal to 20% of the cost of renovating a historic building for use in operating a trade or business or for the production of rental income. These buildings can be either residential or non-residential in nature. The rehabilitation credit offsets income taxes due dollar for dollar.

Are there other things to take into consideration when using this strategy?

There are other considerations related to the classification of renovation costs as either repairs or capital improvements (see Tax Smart Tip #24). In order to qualify for the rehabilitation tax credit, the renovation costs must be classified as capital improvements and depreciated.

There may be situations when the building owner would save more tax dollars classifying the parts of the renovations that qualify as repairs in order to be able to take the immediate tax deduction.

This decision is typically based on the tax bracket of the building owner. If the building owner is in a lower tax bracket but has enough tax to use the credit, this is typically more advantageous. If the building owner is in a high tax bracket and can deduct rental losses, classifying the rehabilitation costs as repairs and deducting them in the year of payment might actually save the building owner more money than the tax credits would.

In this scenario, it is critical to get your accountant involved up front to determine which classification will be more beneficial. Rehabilitation can be planned in such a way as to maximize either classification (See Tax Smart Tip #14). This is just another reason why rental property owners need to tailor their tax strategies (Tax Smart Tip #1)

How do I implement and safeguard the deductions I get from using this strategy?

You implement this strategy by consulting with and engaging a real estate CPA and tax engineering firm during the rehabilitation of the historic building to work in coordination with the architect, engineer and general contractor renovating the building. The CPA and engineering firm document and provide a report of the implementation of the strategy.

Tax $mart Tip #15

Consult your CPA to figure out whether it is more tax advantageous to take the historic building tax credit or to expense the renovation work that qualifies as repairs and deduct it immediately against current year income.

TAX SMART TIP #16
GET A TAX CREDIT FOR DEVELOPING LOW INCOME HOUSING

Description -- Low income housing credits are available to developers and their investors as an incentive for them to build housing for low income families. These credits represent a dollar for dollar credit against income tax liabilities. This credit was not affected by the Tax Cuts and Jobs Act of 2017.

Why is this important?

The government created these credits to act as an incentive for developers to build affordable rental properties. The developers can sell the credits to investors to raise the capital necessary to build these properties. This results in the developer having to borrow less money to build the housing, which allows them to offer more affordable rents to low income families. A win-win all the way around.

What type of properties are eligible for low income housing tax credits?

In order for a property to qualify for consideration for low income housing credits, it must be:

- A residential rental property
- Meet one of two possible low income occupancy threshold requirements
- Restrict the amount of rent in low income units
- Operate under the rent restrictions for 30 or more years

There are two possible low income occupancy threshold requirements –

- The 20-50 rule means that at least 20% of the units must be occupied by households whose income is at or below 50% of the area median income as determined by the Office of Housing and Urban Development.

- The 40-60 rule means that at least 40% of the units must be occupied by households whose income is at or below 60% of the area median income as determined by the Office of Housing and Urban Development.

Rent restrictions relate only to the portion paid by the tenant and can be supplemented by rent paid by local rental assistance programs.

How does the low income housing credit program work?

Every year, the IRS allocates housing tax credits to designated state agencies whose job it is to administer the credit program and award the credits to developers of low income properties.

The credits are allocated to developers based on a competitive process, and give priority to housing that serves the lowest income families and/or serve low income families for the longest period of time.

The credit for a development is calculated based on the cost of development of the property and the number of qualified low income units.

What is the amount and term of the low income tax credit?

A developer (or the investors he sells the credits to for providing cash for the project) receive the following low income housing tax credits:

- 70% of the qualified basis of new buildings if they are not federally subsidized including improvements. These buildings can be new construction or renovated properties that are being converted from commercial to residential use. An example of conversion would be a factory that is converted to residential apartments. The credit is spread out equally over a 10 year period.
- 30% of the qualified basis of a new building that is federally subsidized or an existing building that is not federally subsidized. The credit is spread out equally over a 10 year period.

How do I get low income housing tax credits?

If you are a developer, you apply to the designated state agency in charge of allocating these credits which is available on the HUD.gov website. If you are an investor, you purchase them from the developer by investing in the property.

How do I safeguard my low income tax credits from audit?

If you are a developer, you safeguard your credits by keeping all of the paperwork issued by the designated state agency that awarded you the credits, and you maintain compliance with the rules of the program.

If you are an investor, you safeguard your credits by keeping all of the paperwork you received when you invested in the partnership, which should include documentation of the credits awarded to the developer and sold to you.

TAX SMART TIP #17
USE A SELF-DIRECTED RETIREMENT PLAN
TO BUY REAL ESTATE

Description -- Purchase rental properties using the money in your retirement account as an alternative investment to generate tax deferred or tax-free wealth. The Tax Cuts and Jobs Act of 2017 did not change the rules related to this strategy.

Why is this important?

It offers landlords an opportunity to use retirement funds to purchase real estate which can offer a higher return on investment than traditional stocks, bonds, or mutual funds. It also allows landlords to sell the properties in their retirement account and defer or eliminate the tax consequences.

Who should use this strategy?

Anyone with a retirement account who wants to invest in real estate is a candidate for this strategy. Obviously, the more retirement savings you have, the more opportunities for investment. It is also possible to use a Roth IRA to invest in real estate.

What are the advantages of buying real estate using a self-directed retirement plan?

- Gains on sale are tax free
- Net rental income is tax free
- No mandatory property holding period to get beneficial tax treatment
- Your retirement plan can borrow money to purchase properties, as long as it is non-recourse debt
- You can earn a larger rate of return on your retirement investments

Are there different treatments for borrowing money to purchase properties in various types of retirement plans?

Your retirement plan can borrow money to purchase properties as long as it is non-recourse debt. However, you may run into an issue with UBIT (Unrelated Business Income Tax) as a result. The UBIT tax is levied on

55

the percentage of net taxable income that is considered generated by the portion of the property covered by the loan. It only applies if you have net taxable income after all deductions are taken.

An Example:

John purchased a property using his self-directed IRA for $100,000. He obtains a non-recourse loan of $60,000 to purchase the property. At the end of the year, the property has net taxable income of $10,000. The net taxable income subject to UBIT tax would be $6,000 (60% of $100,000 total purchase price). This percentage is based on the total amount of outstanding debt on the property divided by the purchase price and would change on an annual basis as the loan was paid down.

One way to avoid UBIT tax is to use a self-directed 401K to invest in real estate when borrowing will be used to purchase properties. Self-directed 401K's are specifically exempt from UBIT tax while self-directed IRA's are never exempt from UBIT tax when borrowing is used unless the property does not generate net taxable income.

What types of real estate or real estate related investments can I buy with my self-directed retirement plan?

- Land
- Residential homes (but not for you to live in!)
- Commercial properties - office buildings, shopping centers, industrial buildings
- Apartment buildings
- Condominiums
- Mobile homes
- Real estate notes
- Real estate purchase options
- Tax lien certificates
- Tax deeds

How does investing in real estate with my self-directed retirement plan work?

You can use the following steps to purchase a property with your self-directed retirement plan:

1. Set up and fund a self-directed retirement plan. You can rollover

dollars from other retirement plans as well as contributions to fund your self-directed retirement plan

2. Set up a self-directed retirement plan LLC to give you checkbook control of your retirement funds. Your retirement account owns the LLC.

3. Identify an investment property

4. Purchase the investment property and hold title in the name of the self-directed retirement plan LLC.

5. All rental income must be deposited to the LLC bank account and all expenses paid from the same account. No commingling with personal funds is allowed.

6. All net income and/or gains from sale flow to your self-directed retirement plan tax free. In a traditional self-directed retirement plan, you will not pay income taxes until you begin to draw the money out of the retirement account after you retire. In a Roth self-directed IRA, you never pay income taxes, as the entire retirement account is considered after-tax dollars.

What is a "prohibited transaction"?

Anyone using the self-directed retirement plan strategy must not engage in prohibited transactions. All IRA investments must be made at "arms-length" and you cannot purchase a property from yourself, your business or your relatives with a self-directed retirement plan. In addition, you cannot use the property yourself or rent the property to your children, parents or grandparents.

Are there other rules I must keep in mind when using this strategy?

Using this strategy is a great opportunity to earn tax deferred or tax-free income for your retirement. However, the rules are complicated and as the trustee of your retirement account, you are responsible for knowing all of the rules. Here are some of the big things you cannot do:

- You cannot purchase an investment property from yourself, your spouse, your business or your family members (excluding siblings).
- You cannot use the property for your personal use or rent the property to any family members excluding siblings.

- You cannot collect a fee for managing the property.
- You cannot commingle personal funds with retirement plan funds.
- You cannot run your business from the property owned by your self-directed retirement plan
- You cannot earn a commission or any compensation for buying or selling a property using your self-directed retirement plan.
- You cannot move the property out of the self-directed retirement plan without it being considered a withdrawal subject to income tax.
- You cannot do any repairs or renovation work on the property owned by your retirement plan yourself.

How do I safeguard myself when using this strategy?

Safeguarding your ability to earn tax free income with your self-directed retirement plan involves three basic strategies:

- Keep good records
- Know and obey the rules
- Have a CPA/Tax advisor who knows the rules help you structure your transactions

Tax $mart Tip #17

Buying real estate with your self-directed retirement plan is a great tax strategy for building tax-deferred wealth. There are many rules related to how to do this so make sure you consult with a real estate specific CPA familiar with how to make this strategy work for you.

TAX SMART TIP #18
USE A SELF-DIRECTED ROTH IRA TO BUY REAL ESTATE

Description -- A Roth IRA is a type of retirement plan where the contributions made to the plan are not deductible for tax purposes, but both the income from the plan assets, and any distributions outside the plan, are tax-free.

Why is this important?

A real estate investor can use a Roth IRA to purchase an income property and never pay a dime in taxes on the income generated from the property, or on the capital gain generated when the property is sold.

How is this different from a traditional self-directed IRA?

The rules for self-direction and investing in real estate are the same as in Tax Smart Tip #17. The primary difference between a Roth IRA and a Traditional IRA is that:

- Contributions to a Traditional IRA are tax deductible; contributions to a Roth IRA are not.
- Distributions from a Traditional IRA are taxed upon distribution; distributions from a Roth IRA are not, with minor exception.

Can I convert my traditional IRA to a Roth IRA?

Yes, you can but you will have to pay the taxes on the total amount of the conversion in the year you convert it assuming that all the contributions you made to the Traditional IRA were tax deductible.

The benefit of doing this is that once you pay the tax on the conversion amount, the balance grows tax-free forever and you never pay another dime in taxes again even when you distribute the money to yourself.

Tax planning is key when converting a traditional retirement plan to a Roth IRA. To minimize the tax generated by the conversion, you want to do the conversion is a year where your other taxable income is low or you are taking a tax loss that will offset the income from the conversion.

An example

Trevor wishes to convert $100,000 of his traditional retirement plan to a Roth IRA to invest in real estate. His income from his business is $150,000 every year. However, in 2019, Trevor will be forced to take a $75,000 loss on the sale of a rental property he owns. Trevor would convert his traditional plan to a Roth IRA in 2019.

Result: Because the $100,000 of income generated by the conversion would be offset by the $75,000 loss on the property, Trevor is in a lower tax bracket in 2019 and ultimately pays much less tax on the conversion that he would have if he converted in 2018.

What are the advantages and disadvantages of using a Roth IRA?

The advantages of a Roth IRA are:

- No mandatory minimum distributions at age 70 ½ like a traditional retirement plan
- You can make contributions to a Roth IRA after age 70 ½ if you still have earned income
- You can take penalty free distributions under age 59 ½ for death, disability or for purchasing your first home
- All distributions are tax free including the money you make from buying, operating, and selling a rental property

The disadvantages of a Roth IRA are:

- You are taxed when you convert a traditional IRA to a Roth IRA
- You cannot distribute funds penalty free for five years from the date of the original contribution to the Roth IRA
- You cannot take distributions prior to age 59 ½ unless they qualify for one of the exemptions noted above.

Most financial advisors believe that Roth IRA's are more beneficial than traditional IRA's for the majority of people especially for younger people who have more years of income growth.

Are there limitations to how much money can be contributed to a Roth IRA?

Yes, in order to contribute dollars to a Roth IRA, your modified adjusted gross income on your tax return must meet certain limits and you must have earned income. However, it is possible to bypass the Roth IRA income limits by making a traditional IRA contribution and then converting to a Roth IRA in subsequent years if your income is too high in a given year to contribute. There are no income limitations on converting your traditional IRA to a Roth IRA

An example of the power of a Roth IRA

A client of mine worked for a company for 15 years and when she left the company, she had $100,000 in her 401K plan. She rolled it over to a traditional IRA but was not happy with the returns she was getting on her investments in the plan.

She had an opportunity to purchase an income producing property that needed work but that she felt had a lot of upside for an increase in value. She converted her traditional IRA to a self-directed Roth IRA, paid the taxes on the conversion, and purchased the property for $100,000. After stabilizing the property and filling it with tenants, she had a nice monthly cash flow that went into her Roth IRA. Her return on investment was better than when she was invested in the mutual funds of her traditional IRA.

As a result of her hard work in restoring the property and filling it with tenants, she was able to sell the property two years later for $200,000. For the two years she owned the property, the cash flow into her Roth IRA was $30,000 ($2,500 per month).

So, after the sale, her Roth IRA had $230,000 in it two years after the conversion. She will never pay a dime in taxes on this money and she is free to purchase another rental property and do it all over again. This is the power of using a Roth IRA to invest in real estate.

How do I safeguard myself when using this strategy?

Safeguarding your ability to earn tax free income with your self-directed Roth IRA involves three basic strategies:

- Keep good records
- Know and obey the rules
- Have a CPA/Tax advisor that knows the rules help you structure your transactions

Tax $mart Tip #18

Buying real estate with your self-directed Roth IRA is a great tax strategy for building wealth that you never have to pay taxes on. There are many rules related to how to do this so make sure you consult with a real estate specific CPA familiar with how to make this strategy work for you.

Tax Strategies
When Holding Real Estate

TAX SMART TIP #19
SAFEGUARD YOUR PROPERTY DEDUCTIONS

Description -- Safeguarding your property deductions by maintaining the proper type of documentation and records in an organized fashion. The Tax Cuts and Jobs Act of 2017 presents many opportunities to save money on your taxes but increases the burden on the taxpayer to keep good records to safeguard their deductions. (Tax Smart Tip #2)

Why is this important?

When you own a rental property, there will be expenses that must be paid to finance, hold and maintain the property in good condition. It doesn't matter whether the property is a shopping center, office building, residential apartment building or a single family home; the goal is to generate cash flow without paying income taxes.

The expenses paid need to be tracked in your record keeping system (Tax Smart Tip #4) and proper backup documentation kept for purposes of backing up your expenses so that they are tax deductible. As a general rule of thumb, you should be keeping all of your back-up documentation for three years from the date you file your income taxes and copies of tax returns for seven years from the date you file.

Example #1

Tom files his individual income tax return for 2018 on April 10, 2019. Tom needs to keep the back-up documentation for his 2018 individual tax return until May, 2022. The reason for doing this is that the IRS has three years from the date of filing to audit your tax return.

Typical Property Expenses and How to Safeguard Them

The following is a list of typical expenses that you will incur as an owner of a rental property and the back-up documentation you will need to keep to safeguard your deductions:

- Mortgage interest - interest payments made to a bank or other lender for the purchase and renovation of the property. **Safeguarding documentation** - cancelled checks, loan statements, bank statements, loan amortization schedule, Form 1098 received from lender annually.

- Real Estate Taxes - property taxes paid to local government for services. **Safeguarding documentation** - cancelled checks, bank statements, real estate tax bills, Form 1098 received from lender annually if taxes are escrowed and paid by lender.

- Property Insurance - payments made to insurance companies for protection against damage and liability. **Safeguarding documentation** - cancelled checks, bank statements, insurance bills, Form 1098 received from lender annually if insurance is escrowed and paid by lender.

- Utilities - payments for oil, gas, electric, water, cable and internet for property if not paid by tenant. **Safeguarding documentation** - cancelled checks, bank statements, utility bills

- Advertising - costs of advertising to obtain tenants for property. **Safeguarding documentation** - cancelled checks, bank statements, advertising bills.

- Cleaning and maintenance - the cost of the everyday maintenance of the property including cleaning, landscaping, snow removal and other tasks performed on a regular basis. **Safeguarding documentation** - cancelled checks, bank statements, invoices from service providers.

- Leasing Commissions - the cost of paying real estate agents to find tenants for the property. These commissions are amortized and deducted based on the term of the lease associated with the commission. **Safeguarding documentation** - cancelled checks, bank statements, tenant leases, bills from real estate brokerage company.

- Professional Fees - the cost of paying attorneys and accountants for necessary legal, accounting and tax work related to the operations of the property. **Safeguarding documentation** - cancelled checks, bank statements, bills for professional fees.

- Property Management - the cost of paying an outside company or individual to manage the operations of the property. **Safeguarding documentation** - cancelled checks, bank statements, bills for management fees.

- Repairs - the cost of making repairs to the property as necessary to keep the building systems in operational order. This is such an important area that we will discuss it in more depth in Tax Smart Tip #25. **Safeguarding documentation** - cancelled checks, bank statements, bills from contractors, Form 1099 filed for contractors paid over $600 annually (Tax Smart Tip #23).

- Office Supplies - the cost of paper, toner and other supplies necessary to operate the property. **Safeguarding documentation** - cancelled checks, bank statements, receipts from stores where supplies were purchased.

- Surveys, Appraisals, Title Checks and Property inspections - the costs associated with necessary real estate services when purchasing, refinancing or selling a property. **Safeguarding documentation** - cancelled checks, bank statements, bills from service providers.

- Depreciation - the systematic allocation of the real property portion of the purchase price of the property and the related improvements made to the property expensed annually over the useful life of the property (27.5 years for residential rental property, 39 years for commercial property). This is discussed in more detail in Tax Smart Tips #10, #11 & #12. **Safeguarding documentation** - cancelled checks, bank statements, receipts from contractors doing improvements, Form 1099 filed for contractors paid over $600 annually, purchase closing statements, depreciation schedules.

- Amortization - the systematic allocation of loan costs related to property financing over the term of the loan. **Safeguarding documentation** - cancelled checks, bank statements, purchase closing statements, amortization schedules.

Tax $mart Tip #19

Taking the maximum amount of property related deductions requires good record keeping. You need to implement a system that works for you to track these expenses and use technology to assist you as much as possible. For assistance in setting up a system for tracking expenses, email me at ted@lanzarocpa.com

TAX SMART TIP #20
SAFEGUARD YOUR OFFICE AND ADMINISTRATIVE EXPENSES

Description -- Safeguarding the office and administrative expense deductions by maintaining appropriate, organized documentation and records. The Tax Cuts and Jobs Act of 2017 presents many opportunities to save money on your taxes but increases the burden on the taxpayer to keep good records to safeguard their deductions. (Tax Smart Tip #2)

Why is this important?

When you own a rental property, there will be expenses that must be paid that are not direct property expenses but expenses that relate to the administration and management of the property. It doesn't matter whether the property is a shopping center, office building, residential apartment building or a single family home; the goal is to generate cash flow without paying income taxes and these types of expenses are deductible against your rental income.

The expenses paid need to be tracked in your record keeping system (Tax Smart Tip #4) and proper back-up documentation kept for purposes of backing up your expenses so that they are tax deductible. As a general rule of thumb, you should be keeping all of your back-up documentation for three years from the date you file your income taxes and copies of tax returns for seven years from the date you file.

Example #1

Tom files his individual income tax return for 2018 on April 10, 2019. Tom needs to keep the back-up documentation for his 2018 individual tax return until May, 2022. The reason for doing this is that the IRS has three years from the date of filing to audit your tax return.

Typical Office and Administrative Expenses and How to Safeguard Them

The following is a list of typical expenses that you will incur as an owner of a rental property and the back-up documentation you will need to keep to safeguard your deductions:

- Smart phones, tablets and other technology - the cost of the actual phone or tablet plus the cost of the monthly fees can be deducted to the extent of business use percentage. You may even want to have a business only smart phone separate from your personal one. **Safeguarding documentation** - purchase invoice, monthly fee invoices, cancelled checks or credit card statements used for payment, proof of business usage such as denoting business contacts in phone, taking and storing pictures of properties viewed or pictures of repairs needed.

- Office telephone & internet - the cost of your office landline and internet service related to the management and operation of your landlord business. **Safeguarding documentation** - monthly invoices from service provider, cancelled checks or credit card statements used for payment.

- Computers and other office equipment - purchase price and installation cost of computers, copier, fax machine and other office equipment. The cost of these items are capitalized as fixed assets and depreciated over 5 years and may be immediately expensed (See Tax Smart Tip #12). **Safeguarding documentation** - purchase invoices, invoices from service providers for set-up and installation, cancelled checks or credit card statements used for payment.

- Computer Training - cost of being trained to use computer or specific computer software for purposes of accounting for operations of your properties or making management more efficient or effective. **Safeguarding documentation** -- invoices from service providers, cancelled checks or credit card statements used for payment.

- Office Rent - cost of office space used for management of rental properties, meetings with tenants, contractors and other service providers. If you operate your landlord business from an office in your home, see Tax Smart Tip # 21. **Safeguarding documentation** - office lease agreement, bank statements showing cancelled checks.

- Office Furniture - purchase price and installation cost of desks, chairs, bookcases, tables and other furniture items. The cost of these items are capitalized as fixed assets and depreciated over 7 years and may be immediately expensed (See Tax Smart Tip #12). **Safeguarding documentation** - purchase invoices, invoices from service providers for set-up and installation, cancelled checks or credit card statements used for payment.

- Business related classes and seminars - purchase price and travel related expenses for classes and seminars to enhance your management or operations skills in running your landlord business. **Safeguarding documentation** - purchase invoices, invoices and receipts related to travel, cancelled checks or credit card statements used for payment, documented business purpose receipts for meals and entertainment.

- Membership dues and subscriptions to publications - cost of dues to real estate related associations and cost of subscriptions to real estate related publications including internet based organizations or publications. **Safeguarding documentation** - monthly or annual invoices for dues or subscription, cancelled checks or credit card statements used for payment.

- Marketing and Promotional Items - cost of business cards and other promotional items for purposes of purchasing or selling properties and obtaining outside investors or private lenders for your landlord business. **Safeguarding documentation** - cancelled checks, bank and credit card statements, invoices for services or promotional products.

- Postage - Cost of mailing invoices to tenants, payments to vendors and other mailings related to acquisition, management or sale of your rental properties. **Safeguarding documentation** - cancelled checks, bank and credit card statements, receipts for stamp purchases, mailings, Fed-Ex and other delivery services

- Bank charges - service fees charged by bank for operations of bank accounts related to your landlord business. **Safeguarding documentation** - monthly bank statements

- Meals and Entertainment - costs associated with providing meals and entertainment for prospective tenants, sellers, investors, lenders, and service providers. **Safeguarding documentation** - the best documentation is to keep the receipts from the restaurant for meals or tickets from an entertainment event and then denote who you purchased the meal/ticket for, the business purpose of the meal or event, the date of the meal/event and what was discussed related to business. In addition, keep credit card and bank statements documenting the payment. I would advise you never to pay cash for a business meal or event unless absolutely necessary.

Tax $mart Tip #20

Taking the maximum amount of administrative deductions requires good record keeping. You need to implement a system that works for you to track these expenses and use technology to assist you as much as possible. For assistance in setting up a system for tracking expenses, email me at ted@lanzarocpa.com.

TAX SMART TIP #21
TAKE THE HOME OFFICE DEDUCTION

Description -- Deduct a percentage of your house expenses if you run your rental property business from a dedicated office in your personal residence. The Tax Cuts and Jobs Act of 2017 did not change the rules related to this strategy.

Why is this important?

It allows you to deduct a percentage of your household expenses that you have to pay anyway, but that would normally not be deductible unless you are running a business from your home.

When would I use this strategy?

This strategy is used by rental property owners who manage their properties from a dedicated office in their personal residence. Being "dedicated" means that the room is not used for an alternate purpose when not being used as an office.

The strategy is effective for reducing net taxable rental income on properties.

What type of expenses can be included when calculating the home office deduction that are not ordinarily deductible for tax purposes?

Expenses attributable to a home office deduction include:

- Homeowners insurance
- Utilities - electric, water, gas, oil and wood
- Cleaning
- Maintenance
- Repairs
- Depreciation

The deductibility of these expenses is based on the business use percentage of the home.

71

Are the direct costs of furnishing and decorating the home office deductible?

Yes, all costs related specifically to the decoration and furnishing of the home office are deductible including painting, furniture, area rugs, lamps, book shelves, flooring, other decorative items and office supplies. Some are immediately expensed and some are capitalized as fixed assets and depreciated. (See Tax Smart Tip #12)

How do I determine the percentage of household expenses I can write off using the home office deduction?

Your home office deduction is based on the ratio of square footage between the actual office and the entire personal residence. It is calculated by dividing the square footage of the office by the square footage of the entire personal residence to come to a percentage of business usage.

An example

John and Mary manage their portfolio of rental properties from a dedicated office in their home. The office measures 20 x 15 feet for a total of 300 square feet. The total square footage of the entire personal residence is 1,500 square feet. By dividing 300/1500, you get a business use percentage of 20%. This is the percentage of household expenses you can write-off against your rental income.

How do I track my household expenses to take the home office deduction?

Like all tax strategies, taking the home office deduction requires good record keeping. In order to calculate the home office deduction you would first keep a record of household expenses by month possibly using a spreadsheet or computer software.

At the end of the year, you would have a spreadsheet or computer report that totals your household expenses. You would provide this information to your accountant as part of the total information package necessary to prepare your taxes. Here is an example where John and Mary prepare a spreadsheet of household expenses. The totals can be found below.

John and Mary Household Expenses

	Totals
Mortgage Interest	$ 10,500
Real Estate Taxes	5,000
Homeowners Insurance	1,000
Utilities	1,800
Cleaning	400
Repairs and Maintenance	1,200
Depreciation	2,500
Total	22,400
Business use percentage of home office	20%
Total home office deduction	$ 4,480

My accountant says I should not take the home office deduction because I will have to pay taxes on the depreciation when I sell my home?

This is an old tax preparer myth. The truth is that when you sell your home, you will have to recapture the depreciation taken and pay income tax on it. But, you would have received the tax depreciation deduction and related tax savings for all of the years prior. Since the value of money decreases over time due to inflation and rising costs, you would be saving tax dollars in years where the money is more valuable and paying the taxes years later when the money is less valuable. Plus, you have more money to reinvest in rental properties in the years you are getting the tax savings. Overall, the idea of not taking the home office deduction is a ridiculous argument that is, unfortunately, ingrained in the psyche of many older accountants.

How do I safeguard this deduction?

Maintain the home office space as "dedicated" to your business. Also, you want to prepare the tracking spreadsheet or computerized report and keep copies of all bills related to the expenses noted, along with the bank statements and cancelled checks.

Additionally, there are now numerous apps available to assist you (See Tax Smart Tip #4)

Tax $mart Tip #21

Taking the home office deduction requires good record keeping. You need to implement a system that works for you to track these expenses and use technology to assist you as much as possible. For assistance in setting up a system for tracking expenses, email me at ted@lanzarocpa.com.

TAX SMART TIP #22
TAKE THE MILEAGE ALLOWANCE ON YOUR AUTOMOBILE EXPENSE

Description -- Rental property owners may deduct their automobile usage for any miles driven to manage their properties, look at potential properties for purchase, and for errands related to the management, purchase, or sale of the properties. The Tax Cuts and Jobs Act of 2017 did not change the rules related to this strategy.

Why is this important?

The business use of your automobile for the management of your rental real estate business is a substantial deduction especially for active investors and real estate professionals. It allows you the opportunity to deduct expenses related to your automobile that would not ordinarily be deductible. It requires specialized record keeping in order to safeguard the deduction.

When would I use this strategy?

This strategy is used by rental property owners who have to drive their automobile to manage, purchase or sell their properties.

What type of expenses can be included when calculating the automobile deduction that are not ordinarily deductible for tax purposes?

Expenses attributable to the automobile deduction include:

- Fuel
- Insurance
- Repairs and Maintenance
- Tolls
- Parking
- Registration
- Lease payments
- Interest on auto loans
- Personal property taxes on auto
- Depreciation

　　　　　　　　　　　　　　　　　75

The deductibility of these expenses is based on the business use percentage of the auto.

How do I determine the percentage of automobile expenses I can write off using the automobile deduction?

There are actually two methods for determining what your automobile deduction would be.

- Method #1 involves tracking your business miles versus your total miles driven, calculating a business use percentage and applying that percentage to the actual costs incurred to operate the vehicle.

- Method #2 involves tracking your business miles and applying the IRS's standard rate per mile to the amount of business miles driven to calculate the deduction. The current standard IRS mileage rate for 2014 is 56 cents per mile driven.

- You would compare the deduction calculated using both methods and deduct the greater. For purposes of practicality, method #2 will usually always result in the higher deduction unless you have incurred high repair bills.

An example

John drives significantly to manage his portfolio of rental properties. His mileage log indicates that he drove a total of 15,000 miles in 2018 of which 3,000 miles related to his rental properties. John's total expense for operating his automobile for 2018 was $5,500.

Using method one, John would first calculate his business use percentage - 3,000 business miles divided by 15,000 total miles = 20% business usage. John would then multiply his total operating expenses of $5,500 X the 20% business usage percentage. His total automobile deduction would be $1,100. (20% of $5,500).

Using method two, John would simply multiply the 3,000 business miles by the IRS standard mileage rate of 54.5 cents per mile for a total deduction of $1,635 (3,000 x .545). The IRS standard mileage rate changes on an annual basis and is published annually.

In this example, John would take the higher amount calculated and would deduct $1,635 of automobile expense against his rental income.

How do I track my automobile expenses to take the automobile deduction?

Like all tax strategies, taking the automobile deduction requires good record keeping. In order to calculate the automobile deduction you would first keep a record of daily/weekly business driving. To calculate total miles, I recommend an odometer reading on January 1 and another at year end December 31. A spreadsheet or organizer can be used to track miles or there are now many mileage apps that work with your smartphone that allow you to track mileage and upload the information to your computer to print out a report.

At the end of the year, you would have a report that totals your business mileage. You would give this report to your accountant when providing information to prepare your taxes.

How do I safeguard this deduction?

You safeguard this deduction by maintaining the automobile mileage log and expense records using whatever technology works best for you. Also, you want to keep copies of all bills related to the expenses noted along with the bank statements, credit card statements and cancelled checks used to pay the expenses.

Tax $mart Tip #22

Taking the auto mileage deduction requires good record keeping. You need to implement a system that works for you to track your business and total miles and use technology to assist you as much as possible. For assistance in setting up a system for tracking expenses, email me at ted@lanzarocpa.com.

TAX SMART TIP #23
PROTECT YOUR DEDUCTIONS BY FILING 1099s

Description -- Safeguarding your deductions for repairs, interest and other services by filing Form 1099 annually. The Tax Cuts and Jobs Act of 2017 did not change the rules related to this strategy.

Why is this important?

One of the biggest issues I run into with landlords and real estate investors is failure to file 1099s for their independent contractors and service providers. If you fail to file form 1099 for any of these independent contractors or service providers, you risk the IRS disallowing the deduction for amounts paid for repairs or services.

Who do I need to file a Form 1099 for?

Companies who pay an individual, sole proprietorship, LLC or partnership over $600 for repairs, interest or other services must send that person or entity a Form 1099. For real estate investors, this means sending a 1099 to your contractors, handyman, property manager, and any other person or company who provides services to your business. In addition, you are required to send 1099s for mortgage interest paid to private investors.

If you fail to file form 1099 for any of these items, you risk the IRS disallowing the deduction for amounts paid for the services or loan.

Why don't many investors file Form 1099s as required?

The most common reason for not filing 1099s is that the landlord/ investor does not have the necessary information about their independent contractors and service providers to fill out the Form 1099s.

You can get the information necessary to fill out Form 1099 by having every contractor and service provider fill out a Form W-9. This information includes the:

- Name of person or company
- Address of person or company
- Federal employers identification number (FEIN) or social security number

In many cases, clients are not able to obtain this information because they neglected to have the independent contractor fill out the Form W-9 prior to paying them. Here's an unfortunate fact - Once you have paid an independent contractor (especially those in the construction industry), you will most likely never get their information from them.

What is the solution to make sure you have the necessary information to file the Form 1099?

Make every person/entity that provides your business with services fill out a Form W-9 when you hire them and BEFORE you write them a check.

Why should I file Form 1099s as required by the IRS?

There are several reasons why you need to be able to prepare annual 1099s with accurate information.

1. It's the law. It is simply practical to obey the law.

2. When you file your tax returns for your real estate investments, there are questions related to Form 1099 filings that you need to answer. If you do not answer them, you may be audited. If you answer them incorrectly, you have committed perjury and tax fraud.

3. As mentioned earlier, Filing Form 1099 protects your ability to deduct the amounts paid for the repairs and services. If you are audited and have not filed the necessary 1099s, you can potentially lose the deduction.

Tax $mart Tip #23

Make sure you file your Form 1099s every year to safeguard your tax deductions for repairs and services. You should make every person/entity that provides your business with services fill out a Form W-9 when you hire them and BEFORE you write them a check.

TAX SMART TIP #24
KNOW THE DIFFERENCE BETWEEN A REPAIR AND AN IMPROVEMENT

Description -- Tax laws that went into effect for tax years starting January 1, 2014 created rules regarding the classification of repairs versus capitalized improvements for buildings.

Why is this important?

Repairs are expenses immediately in the year they are incurred and paid for. Capital Improvements are added to the cost basis of the property and depreciated over their useful life (27.5 years for residential property, 39 years for commercial property).

An example

Bob is a commercial landlord who replaces all the flooring his building for $100,000 in 2018. If this is considered a repair, Bob can deduct the entire $100,000 cost of the repairs against his rental income in 2018. If this is considered an improvement, it is added to the cost basis of the property and depreciated over 39 years. Bob gets a $2,600 tax deduction every year for 39 years. This is a huge difference.

What is the effect of the Tax Cuts and Jobs Act of 2017 related to repairs for landlords?

The new tax laws will create both opportunities and pitfalls for building owners. The Tax Cuts and Jobs Act of 2017 did not change the rules related to this strategy but did expand the definition of what types of improvements are qualified for bonus depreciation. (Tax Smart Tip #12)

The Good News!

The IRS regulations that began in 2014 were good news from the standpoint they:

- allow for a better, more lenient definition of repairs
- allow landlords to achieve increased cash flow resulting from lower income taxes
- create an opportunity for business losses related to the abandonment

of building components discarded during renovations (Tax Smart Tip #13)

The Bad News!

The new IRS regulations are bad news from the standpoint that:

- they are complex
- the classification of repairs vs improvements requires careful consideration of the facts and circumstances related to the work being done
- they place the burden of proof for compliance and record keeping on the taxpayer
- they require specialized services be performed in order to take advantage of the repair or abandonment deductibility

So, what is the difference between a repair and an improvement?

A repair –

- Keeps property in efficient operating condition
- restores a property to its previous condition
- Protects the property with routine maintenance
- Includes all minor "incidental" materials and supplies less than $200

An improvement –

- Puts the property in better operating condition
- Restores the property to "like new" condition
- Includes the addition of new property components
- Upgrades or modifies the property
- Extends the useful life of the property
- Adapts the property to a new use

Are there any strategies I can use to make sure I get the repair classification when I have to do work on my properties?

Yes, the classification between repairs and improvements requires the use of judgment and also requires that you keep excellent records to safeguard your repair deduction.

Here are seven strategies that will help you classify work done on your property as a repair for IRS tax purposes -

- Using the guidelines above, have your contractor segregate repairs from improvements on your invoices
- Record the payments as repairs in your accounting system
- Fix only the damaged area that requires repair
- Use comparably priced materials from those you are replacing
- Repair after an event such as a storm, small fire, tree damage, or flood
- Repair during a tenant's occupancy instead of repairing when property is vacant
- Replace less than half of any wall, ceiling or floor, if possible

Remember, in your accounting system, if you call it a capital improvement, the IRS will use that against you and could classify it as an improvement as a result. This would be costly to you as a landlord.

Tax $mart Tip #24

Landlords need to know the difference between a repair and an improvement so that they can maximize the deductibility of the work they do on their rental units. Consult your CPA to maximize your tax savings when renovating a property.

TAX SMART TIP #25
MAXIMIZE THE SECTION 199 DEDUCTION ON YOUR PASS-THROUGH INCOME

Description – The Tax Cuts and Jobs Act of 2017 created a new 20% tax deduction on qualified business income from partnerships, S Corporations and sole proprietorships subject to certain limitations.

Why is it important?

The Section 199 tax deduction is important because it gives real estate investors a 20% tax deduction on the net rental income from their properties. It also gives business owners who run their business as either a partnership, S Corporation or sole proprietorship a 20% tax deduction on their qualified business income. Certain professions not related to real estate are subject to limitations on this deduction but real estate investors involved in brokerage, rehabbing, wholesaling and leasing properties all can benefit from this deduction.

Is my rental income "qualified business income" subject to the 20% deduction?

Yes, it is if your rental property qualifies as a trade or business under IRS Section 162. In order to do that, the taxpayer should be engaged in regular and continuous activity related to the property – basically you manage the property. So, if you are an active investor or real estate professional actively managing a rental property you own, you get a 20% tax deduction on your net rental income.

Example 1

Todd owns a rental property in an LLC. He activity manages the property and his net rental income is $10,000. Todd is entitled to a $2,000 Section 199 tax deduction. Todd will only pay federal income tax on $8,000.

Example 2

Todd owns a rental property in an LLC. He actively manages the property and he has a net rental loss on the property of $2,000. Todd is not entitled to any Section 199 deduction because he has no rental income.

83

This strategy really benefits owners of property that have profits over and above the depreciation deductions allowed to be taken on the property.

What are the limitations that the Section 199 deduction are subject to?

There are income limitations that the Section 199 tax deduction is subject to. The deduction phases out for:

- Taxpayers filing single with income between $157,500 and $207,500 in 2018
- Taxpayers filing joint with income between $315,000 and $415,000 in 2018

The availability of this deduction runs through 2026 and the phase-out limitations are adjusted for inflation annually.

If I am a landlord who also flips properties or has another pass-through business, does the Section 199 tax deduction apply to that income?

The answer is yes, subject to certain rules and limitations. If your business is run as a partnership, S Corporation or sole proprietorship, you are eligible to get the 20% Section 199 tax deduction on your qualified business income.

Example #3

In addition to his rental properties, Todd has a business where he buys, renovates and sells properties. Todd's business is run as an S Corporation. In 2018, Todd flipped 3 houses and made $100,000 of net income. Todd gets a 20% tax deduction ($20,000) and only pays federal income tax on $80,000 of those earnings.

However, there are rules to calculate qualified business income. Todd's salary from the S Corporation that he is required to take under the S Corporation rules is exempt from the calculation of qualified business income.

Example #4

Assume the same facts as example #3 except that Todd has paid himself a salary of $20,000. Todd's qualified business income is now only $80,000 and he gets the 20% deduction ($16,000) on only that portion. Todd ends up paying tax on $84,000 of that income ($20,000 salary plus $64,000 of pass-through income).

What are the tax planning implications of the Section 199 deduction rules?

The tax planning implication of the new rules are immense. The rules are complicated and each taxpayer's individual situation must be reviewed and strategies tailored to maximize the Section 199 tax deduction. There are numerous considerations to take into account such as"

- Am I better off running my business as a single member LLC (sole proprietorship) or as an S Corporation?
- Which is more advantageous – avoiding self-employment tax or getting the maximum Section 199 deduction?
- If I am running my business as an S Corporation, how much salary should I take?
- If I am running my business as a partnership, should my partners and I take guaranteed payments (also exempt from the calculation of business income)?
- If I am above the income limitations and being subject to phase-out of my deduction, should I take steps to reduce my business income using tax planning?

There are many considerations here and this is where proactive tax planning prior to year-end becomes extremely valuable.

Tax $mart Tip #25

If you have net rental income from your properties or you run a business with a pass-through entity or both, you definitely should be doing tax planning prior to year-end to maximize your ability to take the Section 199 tax deduction. For more information on how strategic tax planning tailored specifically to your situation can help you, email me at ted@lanzarocpa.com

TAX SMART TIP #26
USE LLC'S & LP'S TO AVOID RENTAL
PROPERTY AUDITS

Description — Using a business entity like a Limited Liability Company (LLC) or Limited Partnership (LP) not only provides asset protection for your rental properties; it reduces your chance of being randomly audited by the IRS. The Tax Cuts and Jobs Act of 2017 did not change any rules related to using this strategy.

Why is this important?

An IRS audit is akin to a financial colonoscopy. They are no fun, require you to provide a lot of information and will waste a lot of your time and money. This guide is designed to assist you in safeguarding all of your deductions from an IRS audit. An additional strategy is to use business entity types such as the LLC or LP that are audited by the IRS much less than your personal income tax return (Form 1040).

Why does this strategy work?

The IRS audits a much lower percentage of LLCs and LPs than they do personal income tax returns. When you report your rental income and deductions on your personal income tax return, you report them on a form called a Schedule E, which provides the IRS with a detail of your deductions.

The IRS uses this detail to compare your deductions with the national averages for deductions on other rental properties of a similar nature. The IRS calculates a DIF (Discriminate Function System) score for your return. They audit the returns believed have the highest chance of being incorrect and therefore produce the largest amount of tax collected as a result of an audit. This is basically cost-benefit analysis - the IRS choosing to use its audit resources efficiently.

The IRS audits personal income tax returns at a higher rate because of the potential for additional taxes to be paid in. LLC and LP tax returns are flow-through returns, which produce a form called a Form K-1 that provides each partner with their proportional share of income or loss that needs to be reported on the partner's personal income tax return. LLCs and

LPs pay no income taxes. As a result, the IRS audits them at a much lower rate.

How does this strategy work?

A limited liability company (LLC) that has only one member (owner) is considered a disregarded entity for tax purposes, and the income/loss from that LLC is reported on the member's personal income taxes. A LLC must have at least two members to qualify and be reported as a partnership. Typically, married couples will both be members of the LLC to achieve this. Single individuals can partner with a friend, a relative, or create another business entity such as a corporation to be a partner.

A limited partnership (LP) must have at least two partners, one general partner and one limited partner. The general partner is typically the person who will actively manage the property and the limited partner(s) are investors with no responsibility to manage the property. Limited partners are considered passive investors (See Tax Smart Tip #5).

Typically, rental properties are either purchased in the name of the business entity or transferred after purchase into the business entity via a quit-claim deed. Once the property is owned by the business entity, it collects all of the rents, pays all of the expenses and reports the net profit and loss annually on Form 1065 U.S. Partnership Income Tax Return. This return produces Form K-1s for each partner and the net number(s) on the K-1 are what gets reported on the partner's personal income tax return.

The benefit of this is that the IRS has no detailed income and loss information from which to do DIF analysis, only a single income or loss number reported on a different part of Schedule E. This reduces your risk of having a high DIF score and therefore reduces your risk of being selected for an IRS audit.

Tax $mart Tip #26

Choosing the right entity to run your real estate investing business is a must if you want to take maximum advantage of the IRS tax code and reduce your risk of a tax audit.

TAX SMART TIP #27
MAKE NECESSARY ELECTIONS AS A REAL ESTATE PROFESSIONAL

Description -- In order to be treated as a real estate professional for purposes of deducting rental losses, there are specific elections that must be made when filing your personal income tax returns. The Tax Cuts and Jobs Act of 2017 did not change the rules related to this strategy.

Why is this important?

If you recall from Tax Smart Tip #7, a real estate professional is someone who actually works substantially in the real estate business. In order to qualify as a real estate professional, there are certain criteria that must be met on an annual basis.

An IRS Tax trap

In addition to qualifying, you must make certain elections on your tax return in order to get real estate professional status. If you do not make these elections, you will get caught in an IRS tax trap, you will not get real estate professional status, and your losses may be disallowed.

What are those elections?

1. You must elect to be treated as a real estate professional.

2. You must elect to aggregate your properties into one real estate business

Can you give me some examples?

Example #1

Joe spends roughly 600 hours/year in the banking business, but also commits 800 hours managing his rental properties. Since he spends 57% of his time and more than 750 hours/year is devoted to managing his properties, Joe qualifies for Real Estate Professional status.

So, how does this help Joe? It allows for deductibility of all losses incurred from his real estate rental activities against income from his other job, since banking counts as a non-passive source.

However, the Internal Revenue Service has built a trap for investors here. In order for the 750 hours devoted to managing his properties to qualify him, Joe's accountant must have made a tax election on his tax return for Joe to be treated as a real estate professional. If Joe's accountant does not make that election, then current tax law says that the IRS can disallow the losses Joe has taken on his rental properties.

Example #2

Joe has three rental properties that he manages. Assuming the same facts as the previous example - Joe spends roughly 600 hours/year in the banking business, but also commits 800 hours managing his rental properties.

The Internal Revenue Service has laid another tax trap for investors here. Joe's accountant must make the necessary tax election on Joe's return to aggregate each property together as one rental activity. The Internal Revenue Service will deny Joe's status as a real estate professional because he did not spend over 750 hours on EACH property if no aggregation election is made. Joe loses out on deducting his rental losses against his wages and therefore, Joe pays more in taxes than he has to

Individuals who work primarily in a real estate related trade or business can include all hours working in all real estate related businesses to get up to the 750 hour minimum, but they too must make the election to aggregate these activities into one real estate activity in order to qualify.

How do I safeguard my status as a real estate professional?

You must make sure you track your hours managing your properties, working in your real estate business(es), and hours spent in a job or other businesses that are not real estate related. Tracking hours can be done manually or via a time tracking smartphone app. (See Tax Smart Tip #4) In addition, you must make sure that your accountant makes the necessary elections every year to be treated as a real estate professional, and to aggregate your real estate activities into one real estate business.

Tax $mart Tip #27

Make sure your CPA makes the necessary elections every year for you to be treated as a real estate professional (if you qualify) and to aggregate your real estate activities into one real estate business.

TAX SMART TIP #28
PAY YOUR CHILDREN TO DO OFFICE AND PROPERTY WORK

Description -- Increase your property deductions by paying your children to do office work or property maintenance on your income properties. The Tax Cuts and Jobs Act of 2017 did not change the rules related to this strategy.

Why is this important?

Paying your children for work done on your rental properties can increase your tax deductions on your properties if you are an active investor (Tax Smart Tip #6) or a real estate professional (Tax Smart Tip #7).

How does this work?

If you are like most parents, you are already giving your children money in the form of an allowance which is not tax-deductible. But, you can pay your children for work done. Here are some examples of work your children can perform:

At the office

- Filing
- Social Media Marketing (they are probably better at it anyway)
- Creating flyers
- Doing mailings
- Answering the office phone
- Cleaning office
- Any other office administrative functions

At the rental unit

- Cleaning rental units
- Cutting lawns at properties
- Shoveling snow at properties
- Gardening
- Painting

How old must my child be to be paid?

You are allowed to pay children of any age reasonable compensation for any tasks they can perform that are legitimate business functions you would have to pay someone else to do or for tasks that income for the company.

What are the benefits of paying my children to do work in my business?

There are many benefits to paying your children:

1. You are probably giving them money anyway. Teach them work ethic and deduct the amounts you are paying them.

2. You can set them up with an Individual Retirement Fund and make either a deductible contribution (Tax Smart Tip #17) or non-deductible contribution (Tax Smart Tip #18) with the money they earn.

3. If you set up self-directed retirement plans for them, you can make them investors in future rental properties purchased.

4. You can fund their college savings accounts with the money.

The compounding effect of an investment growing tax-free inside a retirement plan or college savings ac-count should result in a nice accumulation of money for them as adults if you start early.

How do I safeguard my deduction for paying my children?

You will need to keep good records on the work performed by the children and how much they were paid for it. Also, you will be required to file payroll tax forms quarterly and annually. Dollars invested into retirement or college savings plans should be documented and account statements kept as verification.

> Tax $mart Tip #28
>
> **This is a great strategy to reduce your income taxes and put money away for your kids.**

TAX SMART TIP #29
TAX PLAN YOUR INCOME TO MAXIMIZE REAL ESTATE LOSSES

Description -- There are numerous tax strategies available for business owners that can help you minimize your business income so that you can maximize your rental property losses. The Tax Cuts and Jobs Act of 2017 created several new tax planning and tax reduction opportunities that must be evaluated when preparing a tailored strategic tax plan (Tax Smart Tip #1)

Why is this important?

This strategy works best for active investors (Tax Smart Tip #6) who are also business owners. It can also work for active investors who are not self-employed. By determining how much earned income and potential rental losses you have in a given year, you can employ various tax strategies to reduce your ordinary income in order to maximize the deductibility of your rental losses.

How do I determine whether year-end tax planning will help me?

You will need to determine:

- What your business income is as of November 30
- What your employment income is as of November 30
- What your rental losses are as of November 30

Once you know this information, it is time to employ some tax strategies to help you maximize the amount of rental losses you can take against your earned income.

What are the different situations you might find yourself in?

Once you have a handle on what your earned income and rental losses are, you will find that you are in one of the following situations:

1. Your earned income is way over the limit for deducting rental losses. Stop right here - this strategy is not for you.

2. Your earned income is slightly over the limit for deducting rental losses or your earned income is causing some of your losses to be

93

phased out. For a married couple filing jointly, rental losses phase out between $100,000 and $150,000 of adjusted gross income. You can reduce your earned income by:

- Purchasing and fully depreciating fixed assets for your business (Tax Smart Tip #12)
- Prepaying expenses in December for the following year to reduce your business income
- Make a retirement plan contribution to reduce your earned income. Employees can make sure they are making the maximum 401K plan contribution to reduce their income from employment
- Deferring any income expected in December into the following year - payments from customers or bonuses from employers can be requested to be paid in January.
- Make a contribution to a health savings account

By using these strategies, you will reduce your earned income below $100,000 and avoid the phase out of the $25,000 of real estate losses you would get as an active investor.

3. Your earned income is below $100,000 but you are showing rental income instead of loss for the year.

You can increase the amount of rental losses for the year by:

- Prepaying your real estate taxes for the following year
- Making an additional mortgage payment on the property
- Making and paying for necessary repairs on the property prior to year end
- Purchasing a new rental property and taking accelerated depreciation on the 5 to 15 year assets (See Tax Smart Tip # 12)
- Prepaying any other property related expenses prior to year end
- Prepaying any other office related expenses prior to year end

These strategies would be especially helpful if you knew that the following year would bring higher income that would phase you out of your rental loss deductions.

How do I know safeguard my deductions using this strategy?

First, you need to remember that these strategies need to be tailored to your situation so you should consult with your tax preparer as to which strategies will best fit your needs. Protecting tax deductions for payment of expenses, retirement plans, and the purchases of fixed assets are all part of good record keeping. (See Tax Smart Tips #2, 19 & 20).

Tax $mart Tip #29

Year-end tax planning to maximize the deductibility of rental losses is a strategy that can save you thousands of dollars annually on your taxes. Contact me at ted@lanzarocpa.com if you would like me to develop a year-end tax minimization plan for you.

TAX SMART TIP #30
OWN THE BUILDING YOU RUN YOUR BUSINESS FROM

Description -- Owning the building you run your business from can save you tax dollars if the business pays you rent. The "Tax Cut and Jobs Act of 2017" did not change the rules related to this strategy.

Why is this important?

Owning the building you run your business from has several advantages –

- It allows you to reduce the amount of self-employment or payroll taxes you pay annually (15.3% social security and Medicare tax including employer match portion)
- The depreciation on the building offsets all or a portion of the rent creating tax-free cash flow (Tax Smart Tip #12)
- It makes your business more valuable when you sell it

How does this strategy work?

You have your business pay rent to you or your rental entity (Tax Smart Tip #26) for the use of the building you own. You must make sure that the rent that you pay is market rent (similar to what you would pay if you rented the building from someone else). Your rental entity pays the expenses of the building and gets a depreciation deduction which offsets the rental income.

Your business gets the deduction for the rent that you pay. Since you are able to deduct the rent, it reduces the amount of income you must pay self-employment on. If you operate your business as a corporation, it saves you on the amount of payroll taxes and corporate income tax you have to pay.

Who should use this strategy?

A business owner who requires a location and wants to convert business income subject to either self-employment or corporate income taxes, to rental income which can be sheltered by depreciation and is not subject to self-employment or corporate income tax.

An example

Jim is a self-employed financial planner who earned $120,000 annually in net business income. If Jim does not own the building he operates his business from, he will pay self-employment tax (15.3%) on the whole amount of net income he earns, or approximately $18,000.

Instead, Jim purchases a house for $270,000 in an LLC to serve as his business office. Annual expenses on the house amount to $15,000 and depreciation on the house is $10,000. Jim pays his LLC rent from his business of $30,000 per year

Result

- Jim reduces his income subject to self-employment tax by approximately $4,500 ($30,000 X 15.3%)
- Jim has net cash flow of $15,000 ($30,000 rent less $15,000 of expenses) and net taxable income of $5,000 ($15,000 net income less $10,000 depreciation).
- Jim only pays income tax on $5,000 instead of $30,000. Assuming Jim's federal tax rate is 20% and his state tax rate is 5%, Jim saves an additional $5,000 in federal and state income taxes every year!
- When Jim wants to sell his business, he will get more money for it because he can sell both the business and the building.

How do you safeguard your rent deduction when using this strategy?

Set up a lease between your business and your rental entity. Make sure that the rent is actually paid every month and that the amount of rent is similar to the amount that would be paid to an outside party (market rent). Check with a commercial realtor to determine market rent in your area.

Tax $mart Tip #30

Owning the building you run your business from works. Remember to set up a lease between your business and your rental entity and pay fair market value rent every month.

TAX SMART TIP #31
FUND YOUR SELF-DIRECTED RETIREMENT PLAN FROM YOUR EARNED INCOME

Description -- Landlords with earned income from a trade or business can fund a deductible self-directed retirement plan contribution from their business and use it to purchase income properties.

Why is this important?

Business owners have the ability to defer profits from their business by making deductible contributions to their retirement plan. There are a variety of options available to do this including self-directed plans which allow you to invest in real estate (See Tax Smart Tip #17). The key is to figure out which retirement plan is best for you in order to both maximize tax savings and achieve your retirement income goals.

Who should use this strategy?

A landlord with earned business income can use this strategy to reduce income taxes by making a deductible retirement plan contribution. There are a variety of self-directed retirement plan options, and each has an annual contribution limit.

What are some of the options available for self-directed plans?

Here are three basic self-directed retirement plan options and their respective contribution limit for tax year 2018 -

- Individual Retirement Account (IRA) - requires you to have earned income equal to or greater to the contribution amount. Maximum contribution for 2018 and 2019 are $5,500 and $6,000 with an additional "catch up" contribution of $1,000 for taxpayers over 50.
- Elective Deferral Plan (401K) - requires you to have W-2 income equal to or greater than the contribution amount. Maximum contribution for 2018 and 2019 are $18,500 and $19,000 with an additional "catch up" contribution of $6,000 for taxpayers over 50.
- Defined Contribution Plan (SEP) - requires you to have earned income. You can contribute 25% of your compensation with a maximum contribution amount of $55,000 in 2018 and $56,000 in 2019.

- Non Deductible Individual Retirement Account (Roth IRA) - You can make contributions similar to an Individual Retirement Account except that they are non-deductible. The advantage is that you never have to pay tax on the income you earn inside the retirement plan as long as you keep it open for five years.

In addition, there may be income limitations on each of these plan types that could reduce the deductibility of the retirement plan contribution. The maximum contributions to each type of plan are set annually based on inflation rates for 2019 and beyond.

How can I use this strategy to minimize my income taxes in conjunction with the other strategies in the guide?

There are several ways to use this strategy to minimize your income taxes while maximizing your ability to use some of the other strategies in this guide such as:

- If you are an active investor, you can use retirement plan contributions to reduce your adjusted gross income and increase your ability to take rental losses (Tax Smart Tip #6)
- You can adjust the amount of deductible retirement plan contribution every year based on your taxable income via annual tax planning (Tax Smart Tip #9)
- You can convert your deductible self-directed retirement account dollars to a self-directed Roth IRA rollover account. You have to pay the taxes in the year of conversion but you get tax free treatment on all dollars earned in the account for the life of the account. (See Tax Smart Tip # 18)
- You can buy real estate with your retirement account and not pay income taxes on your rental income or capital gains until you take the money during retirement (See Tax Smart Tip #17)

How do I safeguard the deductibility of my retirement plan contribution?

You can safeguard the deductibility of your retirement plan contribution by documenting that you made your retirement plan contributions timely. In addition, you should keep copies of the checks used to make the contribution, and the bank statements for the checking account from which the check was drawn on. In addition, you should receive verification from your self-directed retirement plan provider of every contribution you make.

> **Tax $mart Tip #31**
>
> **Retirement plan contributions are a great way to reduce your business income and fund your real estate portfolio.**

Tax Strategies
When Selling Real Estate

TAX SMART TIP #32
KNOW WHAT YOUR GAIN ON SALE IS

Description -- Rental property owners need to know how to calculate the gain or loss on the sale of a property in order to know what the tax effects of the sale are. The Tax Cuts and Jobs Act of 2017 did not change how this calculation is done.

Why is this important?

There are a handful of tax strategy options available to landlords who want to sell their property. In order to know which of these strategies is best for a given sale, you need know whether you have a gain or loss on the sale and how much. Too often, I have seen landlords say to me, "I think I have a loss because I am not getting any money back from the closing" only to find out they have a large gain because of the amount of depreciation they took on the property while they owned it.

When should I use this strategy?

You should evaluate the gain or loss on the sale of a property at the time you receive an offer you may be interested in and PRIOR to selling the property.

What is the correct way to calculate the gain on the sale of a rental property?

The calculation of the gain on the sale of a rental property is formulaic. A spreadsheet that outlines the steps is included in the appendix of the book.

Total Selling Price

The calculation starts with knowing the total selling price. Generally speaking, this is the offer price and can include cash to be received, notes receivable, and the fair market value of any other items received as consideration as part of the sale.

Selling Expenses

Selling expenses are the second piece of the calculation and include all of the expenses of the sale including real estate commissions, transfer taxes, legal fees, title insurance, deed preparation and any other expenses required to close to sale.

Total selling price less selling expenses = net selling price

Adjusted Cost Basis

Once you know the net selling price, you will need to determine the adjusted cost basis of the property. The adjusted cost basis of the property is determined by the purchase price of the property plus any capitalized improvements made to the property during the time of ownership, less the depreciation taken on the property over the time period it was a rental.

original purchase price + cost of capitalized improvements - accumulated depreciation taken = adjusted cost basis

Once you know the Net Selling Price and the Adjusted Cost basis, you can do this simple mathematical calculation:

net selling price - adjusted cost basis = gain (loss) on sale

Realized Gain

But wait, there's more...

If you are not a real estate professional who can deduct all of their rental losses every year, you may have losses from previous years that you could not deduct in those years. Those losses are called passive loss carryovers. They are generated from losses that cannot be deducted because you are a passive investor (Tax Smart Tip #5), or an active investor whose losses exceeded $25,000 in a given year or were phased out because of income in a given year (Tax Smart Tip #6).

These passive loss carryovers can be found on your personal income tax return and are deductible in the year you sell the property against the gain on sale. The calculation is as follows:

gain (loss) on sale - passive loss carryovers = realized gain (loss) on sale

It is from this number that you calculate the income tax or capital gain tax that will have to be paid if you sell the property.

How do I calculate the tax due on the realized gain?

There are various components of calculating the tax due on the realized gain, and this step should be done by your accountant. There are numerous things to consider such as:

- Is there any depreciation to be recaptured?
- How much other taxable income do you have from other sources?
- Are you subject to AMT taxes?
- Do you have any available capital loss carryovers?
- Do you have any available tax credits from other sources that might be triggered with a large gain?
- Will a large gain phase you out of your itemized deductions?
- Is your income high enough to trigger the higher capital gains rates and surtaxes?

With this many variables, there simply is no way to just apply a percentage to the gain. It has to be done with tax software that takes into account your holistic tax situation. The good news is that once you calculate the amount of tax due, you can decide whether it is worthwhile to employ one or more of the Tax Smart tips that follow.

Tax $mart Tip #32

Knowing how to calculate the gain on sale allows you to evaluate whether or not to implement a tax deferral strategy for the gain or simply pay the taxes due.

TAX SMART TIP #33
USE THE PERSONAL RESIDENCE EXCLUSION TO AVOID TAX

Description -- Current tax laws allows for an exclusion of gain on the sale of a personal residence subject to certain criteria. There were no changes to these rules as part of the Tax Cuts and Jobs Act of 2017.

Why is this important?

An exclusion of gain means that you do not have to pay taxes on a gain up to a certain amount. For single individuals, the gain exclusion is $250,000 and for married individuals filing jointly, the gain exclusion is $500,000. This means a married couple can sell their personal residence for up to $500,000 more than their cost basis and never pay a dime in income taxes.

What are the criteria for using the gain exclusion?

In order to use the full amount of the gain exclusion on the sale of your personal residence, you must have lived in that residence for two of the last five years. A partial gain exclusion may be used on the sale of a personal residence if you lived in it for less than two years but had to sell because of changes in employment, illness, or other unforeseen circumstances.

Some examples

Bob and Jane (a married couple) purchased their personal residence in 2014 for $250,000. They live in an area which housing prices have risen dramatically. In 2018, they sell their house for $600,000. They have lived in the house for 4 years so they may exclude the entire gain of $350,000 ($600,000 - $250,000).

Let's assume the same situation except that in 2015 Bob's employer transferred him to another city (an exception to the 2 year rule). They lived in the house for 1 year. They sell the house for $600,000. They can use 50% of the total gain exclusion of $500,000 since they lived in the house for 1 year instead of 2 years. Bob and Jane would be able to exclude $250,000 of gain and would have to pay income tax on the remaining $100,000 of gain.

How can I use this strategy as a landlord or real estate investor?

There are a number of ways to use this strategy as a real estate investor and landlord assuming you are flexible as to your personal housing. Here are some of the strategies that can be used for single family and multi-family properties:

1. You can buy a bargain home in an area where prices are rising and sell it in two years. Any gain under the exclusion amount would be tax-free income.

2. You can live in a house for two years, rent it for three years and sell in within the five year period. Any gain under the exclusion amount would be tax-free income.

3. If you have a single family rental property that is fully depreciated and would have a large capital gain, you can move into it for two years. Any gain under the exclusion amount would be tax-free income.

4. In the case of a two-family house, you could live in each unit for two years within a five year period, rent the other half of the house, and sell it within five years. Any gain under the exclusion amount would be tax-free income.

How do I safeguard my gain exclusion from an IRS audit?

In order to take the gain exclusion, you must document that you have lived in the property for two years. You can do this by having the purchase closing statement, keeping your real estate tax and utilities bills, taking pictures of you living in the house, and keeping track of the purchase and sale dates.

In order to take a partial exclusion based on exceptions to the two year rule, be prepared to document the unforeseen circumstance that forced you to sell and the length of time the property was your personal residence.

Tax $mart Tip #33

Use the personal residence exclusion to avoid paying capital gains taxes on single family or multi-family rentals that you have also lived in for 2 of the past 5 years.

TAX SMART TIP #34
USE A SECTION 1031 EXCHANGE TO DEFER TAXABLE GAIN

Description -- When a landlord sells an income producing property, he may defer the gain on the sale of the property and the related capital gains tax by purchasing a "like kind" property of greater or equal value subject to a series of complex rules. The Tax Cuts and Jobs Act of 2017 did not affect the rules related to this strategy.

Why is this important?

The Section 1031 exchange is the greatest tax tool for building wealth for real estate investors that exists today. The easiest way to build wealth is to not pay any taxes on your investments as they increase in value. Section 1031 allows you to do this thus accelerating the rate that your wealth grows.

When should real estate investors use a section 1031 exchange?

A real estate investor should use a section 1031 exchange when they want to sell an income producing property (rental property) they own and they want to purchase another property of equal or greater value in order to avoid paying the capital gains tax.

When does section 1031 not apply to defer the capital gains on a property?

Real estate investors cannot use section 1031 exchanges to defer gains on properties that were held for personal use, or on properties held primarily for resale. Buying, rehabbing and flipping a property is an example of a property held primarily for resale that would not qualify for section 1031 treatment.

What does "like kind" mean?

A section 1031 exchange is basically just that. The landlord sells one property and purchases another in accordance to the section 1031 rules. This is essentially exchanging one property for another. For purposes of real estate exchanges, the properties sold and purchased have to be held for business or investment purpose but do not have to be identical. For example, you can exchange a residential apartment building for a commercial shopping center or an industrial warehouse for a self-storage facility.

What are the basic rules of a section 1031 exchange?

As mentioned previously, a Section 1031 exchange allows a building owner to completely defer the capital gains taxes due on the sale of a building used in a trade or business, or held for investment as long as they purchase another building of equal or greater value.

In a deferred Section 1031 exchange, the building owner must:

- Identify a replacement property to purchase with 45 days of the sale of the old building.
- complete the purchase of the new building with 180 days of the sale of the old building.
- use a qualified intermediary to hold the proceeds of the initial sale of the property until the new property is purchased. In addition, the qualified intermediary prepares the necessary paperwork to structure the exchange transaction.

A true story (the names have been changed to protect the wealthy)

John is a client of mine who was a plumber. John began investing in real estate by buying small apartment buildings (6 to 12 units). Over the course of 10 years, John used the extra money from his plumbing business to buy about 120 total units. In addition, he purchased a storage warehouse as an investment.

During this initial purchase cycle of John's real estate investments, he lived below his means in a stylish but modest townhouse. He did not spend money unnecessarily and tried to invest as much of his income as he could. At the end of 10 years, John had a substantial net worth and the real estate market in his area had begun to appreciate. John was now in a position to substantially increase his net worth in a very short period of time.

Here's what he did:

John found a large strip shopping center on the main road in his town. It was a bit run down and needed a few new tenants. John sold all of his apartments and his warehouse to another investor and used a Section 1031 exchange to purchase the shopping center for two million dollars. Over the next two years, he fixed up the shopping center and filled all the vacancies. The real estate market was hot. John got an offer to sell the strip shopping center for $4.5 million dollars.

Again, John used Section 1031 to sell the shopping center. In its place, John purchased six retail buildings in Texas rented by a high credit tenant with long term leases. He hired a company to collect the rents and pay the minor expenses related to the property. The tenant was responsible for all taxes, insurance and repairs on the property.

Today, John collects approximately $40,000 a month in net rental income and does absolutely nothing. His properties are worth about five million dollars and he has never paid one dime in capital gains tax on his real estate investments. He took him 10 years to build the base portfolio but once he had it in place, he was able to use the tax code to triple his net worth in a little over 2 years. This is just one example on how Section 1031 exchanges can make you wealthy.

How do I implement an exchange and safeguard it against audit?

When you are selling a property that you have held as an investment, planning is essential. To implement an exchange and safeguard it from audit, you should plan well in advance and consult a tax professional like myself who specializes in real estate investments before the sale occurs because the success of using the Section 1031 strategy depends on the transaction being structured precisely according to the rules.

Tax $mart Tip #34

This is, by far, my favorite tax strategy for real estate property owners, and the one with the greatest wealth building potential. When you are selling a property that you have held as an investment, planning is essential. To implement an exchange and safeguard it from audit, you should plan well in advance and consult a CPA who specializes in real estate investments before the sale occurs.

TAX SMART TIP #35
USE AN INSTALLMENT SALE TO DEFER TAXABLE GAIN

Description -- When a landlord sells an income producing property, he may defer the gain on the sale of the property and the related capital gains tax by giving the buyer a purchase money mortgage (an installment note payable), and receiving the proceeds of the sale on a periodic basis (usually monthly) in the form of a mortgage payment.

Why is this important?

An installment sale is another tax tool for building wealth as a real estate investor. It allows you to defer the payment of taxes over the term of the installment note payable. Since the amount of capital gain tax is based on the amount of the payments received, the installment sale allows you to structure your payments to avoid additional surcharge taxes on taxable income over $250,000 annually.

When should real estate investors use an installment sale?

A real estate investor should use an installment sale when they want to sell an income producing property (rental property) they own, and they do not want to purchase another property but want to maintain a stream of income from the property and defer capital gains taxes.

When does an installment sale not apply to defer the capital gains on a property?

Real estate investors cannot use installment sales to defer gains on properties that were held primarily for resale. Buying, rehabbing, and flipping a property is an example of a property held primarily for resale that would not qualify for installment sale treatment if the investor is classified as a dealer.

What are the basic rules of an installment sale?

When an income property is sold at a gain, the difference between the original purchase price of the property and the selling price is considered to be a capital gain. (See Tax Smart Tip #32). If no tax planning is done, the capital gain tax is all due for the year of the sale.

However, using an installment sale, the seller pays capital gains as they receive payments.

An example:

Bill bought an apartment building in 2014 for $750,000. In 2018, he sells the property for $1,000,000. He gets a down payment of $200,000 and gives the buyer an $800,000 purchase money mortgage at 7% interest with a 25 year amortization and a 7 year balloon payment.

Bill pays taxes on the sale:

- The sales price is divided - 75% ($750,000/$1,000,000) return of purchase price, 25% capital gain.
- The down payment of $200,000 is divided into 2 portions - $150,000 (75%) return of purchase price and $50,000 taxable capital gain.
- Each mortgage payment is divided into 3 portions - taxable interest income for the interest portion of the note payment, the principal portion of the payment is considered to be 75% return of purchase price, and 25% taxable capital gain.

What are the advantages of using the installment sale strategy?

The advantages of using this strategy are four-fold:

- Easier to sell the property during a credit crunch.
- Interest income can be substantial and raises the amount of dollars received on the sale of the property.
- The capital gain on the property is split and partially deferred over a longer period of time, resulting in lower total taxes paid assuming no changes in capital gains rates over the period of the loan.
- If the buyer defaults on the mortgage, the seller can foreclose, keep the payments received including the down payment, and resell the property.

How do I safeguard an installment sale against audit?

To safeguard an installment sale -

- Keep detailed records of the cost basis and improvements made to the property, including the purchase closing statement and invoices for all improvements made.

- Keep a copy of the sale closing statement and the installment note payable document.
- Keep track of all payments received by date.

Tax $mart Tip #35

Use an installment sale when you want to defer capital gains taxes but do not want to purchase another building. You get the cash flow from the mortgage payment without the responsibility of managing the building.

TAX SMART TIP #36
DEFER CAPITAL GAINS BY INVESTING IN A
QUALIFIED OPPORTUNITY FUND

Description – The Tax Cuts and Jobs Act of 2017 created an opportunity for investors to defer tax on prior capital gains (even those not real estate related) by investing in a Qualified Opportunity Fund.

Why is this important?

This new strategy is important because it gives real estate investors another option to defer a portion of the capital gains on the sale of a property without using a Section 1031 exchange (Tax Smart Tip #34) or installment sale (Tax Smart Tip #35).

What is an opportunity zone?

Opportunity Zones are economically distressed areas designated by each state and certified by the Secretary of the U.S. Treasury. Investments in properties in these communities qualify you for preferential tax treatment on capital gains when you invest in them using a "Qualified Opportunity Fund". The purpose of creating opportunity zones for investment is to spur economic development in distressed areas.

What is a "Qualified Opportunity Fund"?

A "Qualified Opportunity Fund" is an investment company set up as either a partnership or corporation that invests in eligible properties located in a qualified opportunity zone. A Limited Liability Company can qualify as a "Qualified Investment Fund" as long as it is taxed as either a partnership or corporation. A "Qualified Opportunity Fund" must invest 90% of its assets in qualified opportunity zone properties.

To become a "Qualified Opportunity Fund", the eligible partnership or corporation self certifies itself by completing a form and attaching it to its federal income tax return for the first year of the company. It must be filed timely which includes extended due dates as long as a valid extension if filed.

What is the advantage of investing in a "Qualified Investment Fund"?

If you invest the proceeds (or a portion of the proceeds) of a property sale that generates a capital gain, you will be eligible to defer paying the taxes on a portion of the capital gain until the property owned by the qualified investment fund is either sold or exchanged or until December 31, 2026, whichever comes first. You have 180 days from the sale of the original property to invest in a qualified investment fund. If you do, the benefits are based on the length of time the underlying property owned by the qualified investment fund is held as follows:

- If the property in the qualified investment fund is held for at least 5 year, you can defer 10% of the capital gains on the funds invested.
- If the property in the qualified investment fund is held for at least 7 years, you can defer 15% of the capital gains on the funds invested.

Example #1:

Charlie sells a rental property he owns for $500,000 in 2018 and as a result has a $100,000 capital gain. He invests all of the $100,000 gain into a qualified investment fund. The fund purchases a property and holds it for five years. In 2024, the fund sells the property.

Result: Charlie does not have to pay any capital gains tax on the sale of his property in 2018 until 2024. When he does pay the capital gains tax, he only has to pay the tax on $90,000 of the capital gain on the original property plus any gain on the sale of the property held in the qualified investment fund.

Example #2:

Using the same scenario, except the fund sells the property in 2025 which is 7 years after if was purchased in the qualified opportunity fund.

Result: Charlie does not have to pay any capital gains tax on the sale of his property in 2018 until 2025. When he does pay the capital gains tax, he only has to pay the tax on $85,000 of the capital gain on the original property plus any gain on the sale of the property held in the qualified investment fund.

- If the investor holds the underlying property in the Qualified Opportunity Fund for over 10 years, then the investor is eligible to receive a step-up in basis to fair market value on the date that the Qualified Opportunity Fund sells the underlying property.

Example #3:

Using the same scenario, except the fund sells the property in 2029 which is 11 years after it was purchased in the qualified opportunity fund.

Result: Charlie does not have to pay any capital gains tax on the sale of his property in 2018 until 2029. When he does pay the capital gains tax, he only has to pay the tax on $85,000 of the capital gain on the original property and he gets a step-up in basis on the property held in the Qualified Opportunity Fund on the date of sale to fair market value which means he has no capital gains on the sale of that property.

How do I find Opportunity Zones?

A list of qualified opportunity zones can be found by using an internet search engine to find "Opportunity Zone Resources" or "Federal Register at IRB Notice 2018-48".

How do I audit-proof this strategy?

First, have your CPA prepare a gain calculation for the property you sold (Tax Smart Tip # 32). Keep all documentation of the sale of your original property that produced the gain. Keep records that you invested in a qualified opportunity fund within 180 days of the sale. If you set up your own qualified opportunity fund to purchase properties, make sure you fill out the form to self-certify and only use the fund to purchase opportunity zone properties. Keep good records of everything! (Tax Smart Tip #2)

TAX SMART TIP #37
DON'T SELL, PASS ON PROPERTY TO HEIRS UPON DEATH

Description -- A strategy that is an alternative to selling your property with large capital gain potential is to transfer the property to your heirs upon your death. The "Tax Cut and Jobs Act of 2017" changed the Federal limit for transferring assets upon death.

Why is this important?

You can completely avoid paying any capital gains taxes ever on the increase in value of an income producing property over a period of time by passing them to your heirs.

Who should use this strategy?

Anyone who has built a real estate portfolio with a total value less than five million dollars can avoid paying capital gains on the appreciation of their income producing property by transferring it to their heirs upon death. It should be noted that individual states may also have estate tax limits which are lower than the federal limit.

How does this strategy work?

Current tax law states that when a property is transferred upon the death of the owner, the heir receives a "step-up" in the cost basis of the property. A "step-up" means that the cost basis of the property becomes the fair market value of the property as of the date of the death of that person, no matter what the owner paid for the property or how much depreciation was taken on the property during the time the dead person owned the property.

The Federal limit for transferring assets upon death is $11,180,000 in 2018. This amount will be adjusted for inflation every year through 2026. State limits may vary but typically state rates are much lower than the IRS estate tax rates.

This means that a property owner can leave up to $11.18 million dollars of assets to his heirs without paying a dime in federal estate or income taxes. The inheritance is not taxable to the heirs until they sell the assets. If planned properly, the heirs will never pay a dime in taxes when they sell either.

An example

John owns an income producing property that he purchased 30 years ago for $1,000,000. Over those 30 years, John has deducted all of the depreciation on the property and now has an adjusted cost basis of zero (Tax Smart Tip 32).

John is ill and has to choose between selling the property and leaving the property to his son via inheritance. The current market value of the property is $2,500,000.

If John sells the property for $2,500,000, he will pay capital gains tax on the entire amount of the sale. At the minimum, he will pay over $500,000 in capital gains taxes.

However, if he leaves the property to his son Sam upon his death, Sam's new cost basis in the property will be $2,500,000. If Sam sells the property a month after his father's death for $2,500,000, he has absolutely no capital gain and he pays no capital gains tax on the sale of the property.

How do I implement and safeguard this strategy?

Estate planning is a complex undertaking (pardon the pun!). It must be planned out using the services of a qualified estate attorney and CPA. It is complicated and must be done correctly. Please consult professionals in this area to implement this strategy. However, if it is done correctly, it can save you hundreds of thousands, even millions of dollars.

Tax $mart Tip #37

This is an awesome strategy but estate planning is complex and must be planned out by using the services of a real estate CPA and qualified estate planning attorney. Please consult professionals in this area before implementing this strategy. If done correctly, it can save you hundreds of thousands, if not millions, of dollars in taxes.

TAX SMART TIP #38
REDUCE TAXES ON GAINS WITH UNUSED PASSIVE LOSSES

Description -- When an income producing property is sold, any passive losses that have not been deducted in prior years immediately become deductible in the year of sale (See Tax Smart Tip #32). The Tax Cuts and Jobs Act of 2017 did not change the rules related to this strategy.

Why is this important?

It is important to remember to account for unused passive losses and to deduct them in the year the property is sold. The passive losses deducted in the year of sale may offset earned income without limit and restriction and therefore are quite valuable.

How does this work?

Passive losses on rental properties can be non-deductible in the current year, because of income restrictions on losses, or because the property owner chooses to not actively manage the property. When this situation occurs, the non-deductible passive losses are accumulated and carried over to future years.

In the year you sell the income producing property, all of the passive losses become deductible in the current year. This is valuable because the losses offset any capital gains on the sale and/or any income earned in that year.

Who should use this strategy?

Rental property owners whose adjusted gross income exceeds $150,000 a year, or who do not actively manage their investment properties.

An example

Robert is a successful manufacturing business owner who owns several rental properties. Robert's business income is $300,000 and therefore, he is not eligible to take any rental losses. All of the losses on his properties are phased out (non-deductible) because of his income. For the past several years, Robert has had losses on his property at 123 Main Street totaling $42,000 which he has not be able to deduct. In 2018, Robert sells the property at 123 Main Street to another investor and has a capital gain of $50,000 on the sale.

Robert will be able to deduct the passive losses carried over from prior years ($42,000) against the capital gain. He ultimately will only pay taxes on $8,000 related to the sale of the property in 2018.

Is there anything else I need to know about using passive loss carryovers?

There are a lot of property owners who own multiple rental properties who aggregate their rental income and expenses on their tax return, instead of reporting the rental income and expenses for each property separately.

If you are a passive investor or someone whose income phases them out of rental losses, then it is imperative that you report your properties separately on your personal or entity tax return, in order to take advantage of the passive loss carryovers when you sell in an individual property.

How do I safeguard my passive losses until the year the property is sold?

Keeping good records that substantiate the rental losses each year, and keeping copies of the prior year tax returns that generated the loss carryforward is always a good strategy.

Tax $mart Tip #38

Report your properties separately if you are a passive investor so you can take the passive loss carryover on that property when you sell it.

TAX SMART TIP #39
LEASE-OPTION TO DEFER CAPITAL GAINS

Description -- Lease-optioning your income producing property instead of selling it is a great strategy that doesn't trigger capital gains tax because the property has not been sold.

Why is this important?

The lease-option is another tool that income property owners can use as an alternative to selling when they are tired of managing the property.

Who should use this strategy?

Any owner of income producing property who has large capital gain potential on their property, but want to defer the taxes for a period of time while maintaining some income stream from the property.

How does this strategy work?

A lease-option is simply a lease with an option to purchase the property at some later date. Instead of selling the property, the owner leases it to someone who wants to manage the property, collects rent on a master lease and allows the investor leasing the property to operate the property.

What are the primary advantages of using this strategy to the owner of the property?

There are several advantages of using the lease option strategy -

- No taxable capital gains because no sale has occurred
- No management responsibilities - the leasing investor operates the property
- Owner maintains a large percentage of the net cash flow after property expenses, and receives an up-front payment for the purchase option which is non-taxable until the expiration of the purchase option.

What is involved in the implementation of a lease option?

The owner of the property leases the property to another investor under a master lease, and gives the investor the option to purchase the property in exchange for a sum of money or other consideration. Typically, the purchase option is for a given price over a certain time period.

The investor leasing the property under the master lease is now responsible for renting out the property, and paying the expenses of the property including the rent due on the master lease. The reason the investor will do this is because they collect a spread of dollars between the rents they collect and the amount they pay out. The leasing investor also typically builds up credits for each payment made towards the ultimate purchase of the property

Ultimately, the investor leasing the property exercises the purchase option and buys the property, or allows the option period to run out and lose their option payment. If the option is not exercised, the owner keeps the option payment and pays ordinary income tax on the amount received in the year the option runs out.

How do you safeguard this arrangement to prevent it from being considered a sale?

The paperwork for the lease-option must be written correctly and good records kept of dollars received.

Tax $mart Tip #39

Use a lease-option strategy instead of selling the property to defer capital gains and maintain cash flow from the property without management headaches.

About The Author

Theodore D. Lanzaro is a Certified Public Accountant, real estate investor, real estate broker, author and speaker with over two decades of real estate tax consulting and investing experience. He is the founder of Lanzaro CPA, LLC located in Cheshire, Connecticut, a boutique CPA firm specializing in accounting and taxation for the real estate industry. For the past 28 years, he has helped thousands of real estate business owners, entrepreneurs and investors all over the United States implement cutting edge tax strategies that save them thousands of dollars annually on their taxes.

Mr. Lanzaro has made numerous appearances on various television and radio shows including Fox Business News to discuss current tax topics. He has also contributed to articles that appeared in Investor's Business Daily, the Wall Street Journal and a variety of other local Connecticut newspapers.

Mr. Lanzaro is the author of "The Tax Smart Landlord" and "The Tax Smart Landlord" toolkit as well as over 100 articles on taxation for the real estate industry specifically for investors, landlords, "flippers", and developers.

Ted is a sought after speaker and has spoken all over the United States to groups of real estate investors and business owners on the taxation of real estate.

For more information about CPA Ted Lanzaro, you can visit his website at **www.lanzarocpa.com**

Bonus Offer

I would like to offer you a Free Bonus Report for reading my book. The Free Bonus Report entitled:

The Tax Smart Landlord Guide to Evaluating Rental Property Purchases

This is my special report on how to financially evaluate a rental property. This report shows you how to calculate net operating income, cash flow, capitalization rate, cash on cash return on investment and a variety of other financial ratios you need to accurately evaluate the investment potential of a rental property and includes a property evaluation spreadsheet that automatically calculates it all for you.

It can be downloaded for free at www.taxsmartlandlord.com/bonusreport

Appendix

Tax Smart Tip #8 – 2018 Tax Brackets

Tax Smart Tip # 11 – List of Land Improvement Items with 15 Year Useful Life

Tax Smart Tip # 11 – List of Tangible Personal Property Items with 5 Year Useful Life

Tax Smart Tip #32 – Realized Gain on the Sale of a Property Calculation

2018 BRACKETS

Rate	Single	Married Filing Seperately	Married Filing Jointly	Head of Household
		Taxable Income over...		
10%	$0	$0	$0	$0
12%	$9,525	$9,525	$19,050	$13,600
22%	$38,700	$38,700	$77,400	$51,800
24%	$82,500	$82,500	$165,000	$82,500
32%	$157,500	$157,500	$315,000	$157,500
35%	$200,000	$200,000	$400,000	$200,000
37%	$500,000	$300,000	$600,000	$500,000

Schedule of 15-Year Direct Land Improvements

Date purchased: ____ / ____ / _____ Date placed in service: ____ / ____ / _____

Property type: _____

Property address: _____

Land Improvement Items	Number of Units	Value Per Unit	Total Cost
Bridges			
Canals			
Curbs			
Docks			
Drainage, underground pipes & drains			
Fences			
Landscaping/trees			
Curbs			
Driveways			
Roads			
Sewers - non-municipal			
Shrubbery			
Sidewalks			
Sprinkler systems			
TV/radio transmittal towers			
Waterways			
Connected with any land improvements:			
Electrical			
Grading			
Plumbing			
Lighting			
Other ancillary:_____			
Total 15 Year Land Improvements			

Schedule of 5-Year Tangible Personal Property

Date purchased: ____ / ____ / _____   Date placed in service: ____ / ____ / _____

Property type: _____

Property address: _____

Description	Number of Units	Value Per Unit	Total Cost
Appliances:			
Dishwasher			
Clothes Dryer			
Garbage disposal			
Microwave Oven			
Stove/Oven			
Refrigerator			
Trash compactor			
Wine Cooler			
Window air conditioning			
Other appliances:_____			
Antennas and antenna towers			
Awnings & canopies			
Billboards			
Blinds, drapes, shades			
Boat slips (floating docks)			
Coin-operated laundry equip.			
Carpeting (not glued down)			
Other removable floor coverings			
Counters, cabinets, racks, shelves			
Dehumidifiers			
Emergency generator			
Exhaust fans			
False balconies			

Description	Number of Units	Value Per Unit	Total Cost
Fans			
Fire extinguishers			
Flagpoles			
Furniture - inside & outside			
Glassware, silverware, kitchen utensils			
Greenhouse			
Heater			
Heaters - plug-in unit heaters			
Heaters - space heaters			
Heat lamps			
Hot water heaters, hot water lines			
Light fixtures			
Mirrors			
Ornamental fixtures			
Outdoor advertising signs			
Plants			
Personal library			
Pole signs			
Poles			
Refrigeration equip./units			
Roll-up doors			
Safe			
Safety equip.			
Safety Doors			
Sheds (movable)			
Signs			
Signs, neon			
Signs, rooftop			
Storage bins/facilities			
Storage tanks			
Sump pump			
Suspended ceilings			

Description	Number of Units	Value Per Unit	Total Cost
Telephone equip.			
Trailers (mobile homes)			
Toilets			
Tubs			
Vanities			
Vault door			
Vault			
Vending machines			
Walk-up & drive-up bank tellers window			
Wall partitions - movable, removable			
Wall partitions - non-weight bearing walls			
Wall panel inserts			
Walk-in freezers/coolers			
Window washing equip.			
Other:_____			
Electrical connected with any personal property			
Plumbing connected with any personal property			
Other ancillary connections:_____			
Total Personal Property			

Realized Gain on the Sale of Property
Calculation Worksheet

Basic Computation of Realized Gain	$	
Total Selling Price		
Less: Selling/Closing Expenses (from closing statement)		
Net Selling Price		
Less: Cost Basis of Property (see below)		
Gain on Sale		
Less: Passive Loss Carryovers (from your tax return)		
Realized Gain on Property	$	
Calculation of Cost Basis of Property		
Original Purchase Price		
Plus:		
Closing Costs from Purchase		
Cost of Improvements Made on Property		
Less:		
Accumulated Depreciation Taken on the Property		
Cost Basis of Property		

www.ingramcontent.com/pod-product-compliance
Lightning Source LLC
Chambersburg PA
CBHW060611200326
41521CB00007B/733